PENGUIN BOOKS

Crying in the Dark

Shane Dunphy was born and brought up in Wexford where he now lives. He has worked as a child-protection worker in several countries and now teaches childcare courses in Waterford. *Wednesday's Child*, his first book, was a bestseller. He is a regular contributor to the *Irish Independent*.

Crying in the Dark

SHANE DUNPHY

PENGUIN BOOKS

PENGUIN IRELAND

Published by the Penguin Group

Penguin Ireland, 25 St Stephen's Green, Dublin 2, Ireland (a division of Penguin Books Ltd)
Penguin Books Ltd, 80 Strand, London WC2R ORL, England
Penguin Group (USA) Inc., 375 Hudson Street, New York, New York 10014, USA
Penguin Group (Canada), 90 Eglinton Avenue East, Suite 700, Toronto, Ontario, Canada M4P 2Y3
(a division of Pearson Penguin Canada Inc.)
Penguin Group (Australia), 250 Camberwell Road, Camberwell, Victoria 3124, Australia
(a division of Pearson Australia Group Pty Ltd)
Penguin Books India Pvt Ltd, 11 Community Centre, Panchsheel Park, New Delhi – 110 017, India
Penguin Group (NZ), 67 Apollo Drive, Rosedale, North Shore 0632, New Zealand
(a division of Pearson New Zealand Ltd)
Penguin Books (South Africa) (Pty) Ltd, 24 Sturdee Avenue,
Rosebank, Johannesburg 2196, South Africa

Penguin Books Ltd, Registered Offices: 80 Strand, London WC2R ORL, England

www.penguin.com

First published by Gill & Macmillan 2007
Published in paperback in Penguin Books 2007

1

Set in 12.5/14.75 pt Monotype Garamond
Typeset by Rowland Phototypesetting Ltd, Bury St Edmunds, Suffolk
Printed in England by Clays Ltd, St Ives plc

A CIP catalogue record for this book is available from the British Library

ISBN: 978-0-141-03135-4

Fare you well, my own true love,
Farewell for a while
I'm going away, but I'll be back
If I go ten thousand miles
Ten thousand miles, my own true love
Ten thousand miles or more
The rocks may melt and the seas may burn
But you know that I'll return
Oh don't you see the lonesome dove
Sitting on an ivy tree
She's singing a song for her own true love
As I shall sing for thee
Oh come you back my own true love
Come back and stay a while
If ever I had a friend at all
You've been a friend to me
Fare you well, my own true love,
Farewell for a while
I'm going away, but I'll be back
If I go ten thousand miles

'*Ten Thousand Miles*',
TRADITIONAL FOLK SONG

Contents

Preface

Crying in the Dark is the second part of a story begun in another book, *Wednesday's Child*, but can be read as a stand-alone – the narrative recounted here is not dependent on a reader having first read the previous title. This volume deals with different children in a different setting, and takes up the narrative twelve months later.

The incidents I write about have been taken from across the fifteen years I worked in child protection, and have been compressed into a three-month timeline for ease of reading. They did not happen concurrently, and names, gender, ages and all other identifying details have been altered to protect the identities of those described. The story you have before you takes place in a city, in Ireland, over a summer some time within the recent past; *that is simply the setting.* It could have occurred anywhere at any time. Everything did, however, happen. The events are all true.

The workers I describe in this book, other than myself, are purely fictitious, composites of people with whom I have worked. I have reproduced procedure as closely as I can, but different regions operate different procedural methods, so what you read here may differ slightly from your personal experience. I have tried to leave jargon and technical language out of the text as much as possible. Where it does occur, I have explained its meaning as simply as I can.

PART ONE

Standin' at the Crossroads

I'm standing at the crossroads and I don't know where to go;
The sun is gettin' higher and my heart is filled with woe.
I hear the wind a-moanin' and the dust is gettin' high,
But I'm standin' at this crossroads and the devil's passin' by.

'Standin' at the Crossroads', TRADITIONAL BLUES SONG

I

The flats loomed out of the scutch grass and scrub of the wasteland like towers from a doomed kingdom. The land all about us was dotted with the husks of burnt-out cars, skeletons of twisted, mythological beasts. Stocky, piebald horses grazed on the reeds and tough vegetation with a dissatisfied look on their long faces, halters of blue, synthetic rope about their noses. A cloud of smog hung low over the twin keeps, foreboding in the rapidly approaching dusk. I lit a cigarette and handed the Zippo to my companion, Bill Creedon, a city Garda, tonight dressed in plain clothes.

'D'you think he's in there?' I asked, puffing smoke from the corner of my mouth, as Bill flicked the lid of the lighter closed and handed it back to me.

'Oh, he's there all right,' he said. 'C'mon. He's had too much of a head-start already. I'll take the rear entrance, you take the front.'

I was working in a residential home for teenage boys, many of whom had been sent to us by the courts, having fallen foul of the law for an assortment of offences, anything from drug-dealing to joy-riding. I was there on a temporary basis, looking for something more permanent, but not searching too hard. I was really only dipping my toes back in the waters of childcare after a year's break. On weekdays I taught at a local college, and

3

I worked at the unit one night mid-week and at weekends. To judge from my performance so far that night, they would not be rushing to offer me a permanent post in the near future.

Roger, a new arrival who was supposed to be under my watchful eye, had made good his escape after only an hour in our care, breaking a bathroom window on the second floor of the building and climbing onto the roof, then down a fire-escape. It was the oldest trick in the book. Because we had an extra staff member on duty that night (we always did when there was a new child coming in), I had been sent out with the local police to bring him back. Bill, the juvenile liaison officer from the closest station, was used to our calls and had agreed to act as guide.

This had been Roger's first time in care, so he had not been difficult to track. A more experienced child would not have headed for home, but would have laid low somewhere for the first few hours, and then gone to a friend's house – somewhere we, or the police, would not have known about. Roger, on the other hand, had beaten a path straight for his mother's place in the Oldtown flats.

Bill and I walked over the hilly, pocked ground. We had been spotted from a good distance away. Children on bikes halted and watched us approach. Teenagers, lounging on the fence that separated the flats from no man's land, looked up and followed us with sullen attention. I glanced over at my companion. Although he was dressed similarly to me – a loose-fitting T-shirt, jeans and work-boots – he exuded the pungent aroma of 'cop'. I didn't know whether it was his close-cropped hair, his stocky, muscular build or the way he held himself, but there was no doubt about his profession. Even if I had not known him, I could have picked him out of the crowd in any bar as a Guardian of the Peace. The group of kids awaiting us had already done so. I was probably a puzzle to them, but the fact that I was in the company of the enemy made me an unwelcome visitor.

We passed through a jagged gap in the metal fence and arrived at the base of the towers.

'Meet you in the middle,' Bill said and kept walking without pause around the corner of the building.

The towers had not been built with much architectural imagination. They were simply two six-storey rectangles of grey concrete, each containing thirty small flats, intended for families on the public housing list. Built more than twenty years earlier, they had become a ghetto of crime, wasted lives and human degradation. Someone involved in urban planning had apparently forgotten that sticking sixty families with a multitude of social problems into cheaply built cages, without any support network, was effectively inviting the gangs and the local mobsters to set up shop in the area. And, to the utmost surprise of the local authority, that is exactly what had happened.

Roger was a child of this environment. He had been born in the flats to a single-parent family and had become immersed in a life of petty crime and violence almost as soon as he could walk. He was now sixteen, and it would have been comforting to think that professionals like Bill and me could have done something for him, but it was unlikely that the trajectory of this young life would be altered. However, we would try. That was our job.

I started up the stairs. On the second landing a group of young men were sharing a joint. They watched me pass and said nothing, but their eyes followed me with naked threat. I knew that I was deep in alien territory, and was glad that Bill was nearby.

Roger lived on the third floor. As I came out of the stairwell onto the landing, I heard a shout from the group below.

'Rog, you're busted! Get outta there!'

Roger, who must have been waiting for such a cry, barrelled past me. I dropped my cigarette and took off after him. Bill was coming up the stairs at the end of the landing – I had climbed up the middle – but there was another flight at the other end, and this was the one down which Roger had gone. Bill and I pounded after him.

We hit the pavement outside the flats in time to see our charge vanishing around a corner and down an alley about a hundred yards away.

'He's heading into Oldtown village,' Bill panted. 'You go after him. I'll try and cut him off from the other end. He'll head for Main Street.'

I worked on the premise that, although Roger was faster, I was fitter and would eventually wear him out. What I hadn't banked on was the terrain we were running across. He took me on a tour of alleyways and back streets, a crazy, ragged path that went over fences, across walls and through piles of rubbish and junk. It was like running an obstacle course constructed by Oscar the Grouch, and by the time we had emerged into the main city thoroughfare again, I was drenched in sweat, reeking of dirt, and my muscles were aching in ways I had never imagined possible. I paused and pondered the only possible path Roger could have taken.

The alley gaped, dark and filthy, like the dry bed of some foul river. I stood before it, leaning against a grime-stained wall, catching my breath. I heard movement in the darkness and knew there was nothing for it but to go into the shadows.

'Roger, is that you?'

The city buzzed and pounded about me as if it was the heart of an enormous beast. Sweat trickled down my forehead and into my eyes. Ireland is not a warm country. It is usually wet and intemperate, but this had been the hottest summer I had known. The night air was heavy and felt like treacle as I sucked it in and out of my lungs.

I had been close behind Roger, and there was nowhere else to go than up the narrow passageway. I called again, and my holler was answered only by more shuffling and what sounded like a can being kicked. I peered into the gloom and began to slowly pick my way through the scattered rubbish towards the source of the noises.

The alley smelled of urine and stale cider. The deeper in I went, the farther away from reality I seemed to be, as if the rest of the world was getting distant. The sounds of traffic and human life from the street seemed to grow faint and dim. I was wrapped in darkness, sodden heat and human waste.

'Roger, come on, man. Enough is enough. Let's go back and get cleaned up.'

I heard shuffling footsteps and then made out huddled shapes at the end of the alley. There were four of them, but I couldn't tell if Roger was one of them or not. They had their backs to me and were leaning over something. I got the sickening sense that they were feeding; there was an aura of almost frantic hunger to them.

'Hey,' I called from several feet away.

One turned, and I saw pale eyes set in a wizened face, a gash of a mouth and green, cracked, broken teeth.

'Go 'way, you,' the man drawled. 'There's nothin' for you here.'

I could smell the sickly aroma of cheap wine from him. Then a muffled cry that was nearly a sob drifted up from among them, and I knew where the boy was. Panicking, I lunged forward, grabbing the closest one by the shoulder and spinning him away. Roger was sprawled on the ground, surrounded by the winos, his hoody half off and a look of abject terror on his face. I did not know if they were stealing from him or doing something worse, but there was no time for questions. I reached down and dragged Roger to his feet.

'Leave him alone,' I said, hearing the tremble in my voice as we backed away.

They closed ranks, shuffling slowly together, a line of blank eyes staring at us. They were of indeterminate age – they seemed old, but with their rags and dirt-smeared faces they could have been younger than my thirty years. I pushed Roger behind me and took out my mobile phone.

'The cops are nearby,' I told them. 'I'm calling them right now, so don't move one fucking step.'

They came at us in a rush before I had a chance to dial, displaying a speed of movement that they should never have possessed. Roger screamed and ran, breaking out of my grip and shooting away towards the relative safety of the street. I had time to aim a kick at the closest groin and then they were on me. I went down on my back with a thud and cracked my head on the ground. Stars exploded across my vision. A fist hit me full on the nose. More stars, and awareness began to drift. I fought to wrest it back, but it was a losing battle. I punched blindly, connected with something soft, and then knew nothing for a time.

The feeling of nausea woke me.

I tried to open my eyes, but when I did the sky spun and pin-wheeled and then the sickness overpowered me and I rolled over and vomited a great gush onto the concrete. After getting sick again, I felt a little better. It occurred to me that I was on all fours, like a dog, and I crawled away from the pool of puke, finding a clear spot to sit down. I reached into the pocket of my jeans for my phone, but it was gone. My wallet too. A quick glance at my feet informed me, with some relief, that my boots were still there. Using my hands to grip the rough face of the wall behind me, I was dragging myself to a semi-standing position when I heard voices at the mouth of the alley. I groaned. If this was more trouble, I was in no condition to deal with it. Hell – I had not dealt with the last lot particularly efficiently.

'Shane?'

'Bill, I'm here.'

He winced when he saw me.

'Christ, what happened to you?'

'I got jumped. I made the mistake of flashing my

mobile phone at a bunch of homeless people. I might as well have asked them to mug me. I take it you lost our young friend.'

'He showed us a clean pair of heels. Listen, I'm taking you to the hospital. Is your nose broken?'

I touched it tenderly. 'No, I don't think so.'

Bill helped me to get up. My head swam for a second and I had to lean on him, but then it cleared and I was able to stand unassisted. I felt the back of my head. There was a large lump, but the skin wasn't broken.

'I'm okay. Just lead me back to the unit. A few paracetamol and a shower and I'll be fine.'

'Don't be an arsehole. You've probably got a concussion.'

'There's a nurse on the staff. I'll be seen quicker there than if I go to Casualty, *and* there's less chance of being mugged a second time'.

'Well, I can't argue with that. My car's near. Can you walk?'

'I'll manage.'

Back at the unit, I was fussed over and patched up by Jacinta, the nurse, and sent to bed immediately with a dose of painkillers. I didn't complain. The clients were all asleep, and if there were any disturbances during the night I would be called.

As it happened, I slept without being woken, and at eight thirty the next morning was sitting in the office, sipping coffee, nursing a mild headache and writing up the incident report of the previous night's adventure. I left out the full details of my encounter with the transients, because it had no bearing on Roger's continued absence, and because I was deeply embarrassed at having been overwhelmed by a bunch of drunks. I simply indicated in the report that there had been a scuffle that had detained me long enough for the wily youngster to elude me. I was just signing and dating the report when Jane, the house manager, came in.

'Shane, I was hoping to have a word with you.' She poured herself a mug of coffee and sat down in the chair opposite me. 'Eventful evening?'

'So so.'

'That's not what I heard.'

'If you've come to gloat, you'll have to get in line.'

'Actually, I wanted to discuss something with you. You're looking to get back into childcare full time, aren't you?'

'Well, I'm considering it, yeah.'

'I got a call last night from an old boss of mine, Benjamin Tyrrell.'

'Ah, Ben. Yeah, I did a bit of work with him a few years back.'

Tyrrell was well known in childcare circles in Ireland as a charismatic leader, and something of a maverick. He had been one of the first managers of a residential child-care unit in the country who was not a member of a religious order, and he tended to divide opinion right down the middle: he was either loved or loathed. I had a deep fondness for the man.

'He's running some kind of outreach programme for children with special needs,' Jane said. 'He's just been appointed. I think the project is financed by one of the voluntary agencies. He didn't give me many details, but the kids are, shall we say, extremely challenging. Ben had heard that you were helping out here, and wondered if you'd be interested in jumping ship.'

Benjamin was always interesting to work with. His ideas were fascinating, he was a naturally gifted manager, and he was one of the most talented childcare workers I had ever encountered. Children simply opened up to him. I had been drifting for the past twelve months. I enjoyed the teaching, but was not fully committed to it. Similarly, I knew that I was not cut out for work with young offenders. Jane knew it too.

'I think this is what you've been waiting for, Shane. We'll be sorry to lose you, but –'

'No, you won't,' I said with a smile. 'I appreciate your taking me on, but this isn't me, and we both know it. I'll tell you what. Give me Benjamin's number and I'll see what he has in mind.'

She pulled over a notepad and scribbled down a number.

'He'll be there all day, and is looking forward to talking to you. It sounds like a really good opportunity. If I were you, I'd go for it.'

I tore out the page and put it in my pocket.

I phoned Benjamin when I got home later that morning, but he was not available. The phone rang an hour later, just as I was about to go to the gym. It was the administrator from the project.

'Mr Tyrrell asked me to call you back. He wonders if you might be able to come out to see him?'

I said that I would and wrote down the address.

The project was based in a big, grey, stone house, built in the early part of the twentieth century. A bronze plaque on the wall said 'Dunleavy House'. It was on a pleasant, tree-lined avenue in a quiet part of the city. Lawyers and accountants also had offices on the street, but some decent people probably worked there too. Across the road was a green area of well-tended trees and bushes with a pond in the centre. Inside, a lobby held a small desk, behind which sat a stern, grey-haired woman at a computer. A name-plate on the desk declared her to be Beverly Munro, Trust Secretary. She looked at me disapprovingly. Looking the way I do (like a refugee from the Grateful Dead), I get a similar response a lot.

I introduced myself, told her why I was there, and in a few seconds Benjamin was standing in front of me.

He was around the same height as me, with a slighter build, and greying, longish hair that had once been dark brown. He wore John Lennon-style, circular, wire-frame glasses and had a goatee beard. I knew that he was fifty-three years old, but he could have easily passed for ten years younger. He was dressed in brown corduroy trousers, a green shirt and a grey waistcoat. His eyes were his most striking feature: they sparkled with intelligence, good humour and warmth, but I could never pin down what colour they were. Sometimes they seemed to be brown with green flecks, but in a different light they could appear almost blue.

They were as mercurial as his personality. I had never been on the receiving end of his temper, but during a previous work engagement I witnessed him verbally dismember a social worker who was purposefully stalling the foster placement of one of our children. She had, it turned out, favoured another child on her books, a child much more troublesome and far less suited to the family in question. Benjamin conducted an object lesson in the martial use of language, and in so doing reminded me that, while a gentle and sensitive man most of the time, he could be a formidable opponent and was not someone to get on the wrong side of.

He cared passionately about the children in his care, and did not suffer individuals who were less dedicated to the cause than he was. While most managers worked from nine to five, it was not unusual for Benjamin to be still at whichever house he was running at midnight. This meant that he had risen to almost legendary levels within the Irish social-care system, his ideas actually being taught on third-level courses, but his personal life was effectively non-existent. He spoke to me once of a failed marriage in his youth, and he had no children, other than those he worked with, many of whom remained in contact with him long after leaving care. I knew from experience that Benjamin was as hard on himself as he was on his staff. He expected a hundred per cent commitment from everyone. If I decided to take the job, I would be working with a unified, dedicated team of people. Benjamin Tyrrell was the best, and he expected the best.

'Shane, my boy. Good to see you!'

He flung his arms around me. I laughed despite myself. I had forgotten how physically expressive he could be.

'Ben, it's really good to see you too.'

'What happened to your nose? I had heard you'd finally started looking after yourself.'

'It's a long story I'd rather not go into just now. Tell me you have coffee brewing somewhere.'

'I've got some gunpowder green tea. You'll love it.'

'I never really kept up the whole herbal tea thing, Ben. I'm back on coffee. *Lots* of coffee.'

'Java will kill you. This way, you get the caffeine and a lot of stuff that is actually good for you.'

'Really?'

'Well, so I'm told anyway. I'm giving it a go. Let's see if we can't convert you.'

He led me through the door and down a narrow corridor to a well-lit and comfortable office. A white teapot was on the desk, and he poured two cups.

'So,' he said, 'tell me what you've been up to since I saw you last.'

He turned his clear gaze upon me, and I found myself squirming under it. I suddenly wondered why I had come. I didn't even know if I wanted what Ben was offering. I had messed up the job at the unit terribly, and had fled my last full-time childcare post because I just could not do the work any more – it hurt too much. My confidence was at an all-time low. I felt like a fraud.

'This and that.'

'Mmm. You're working with young offenders at the moment, I hear.'

'It's just part time. I'm teaching at a community college. I'm on summer holiday right now, so I'm doing a few extra hours for the unit. They need the help. Staff turnover is high. It's tough work.'

'Do you want to come back to childcare?'

He'd cut right to the chase. I was actually relieved.

'I don't know. I left it almost a year ago because . . . because I didn't want to do it any more. I was getting too involved with some of the cases and my personal life was suffering. It probably wasn't great for the children either. So I wrapped up what I could, and I got out.'

Benjamin nodded and produced a tobacco tin from his breast pocket. He cocked an eyebrow at me to ask if I minded. I shook my head. He began to roll one.

'And yet you're back at the coalface.'

'I saw an advertisement for temporary staff at the unit. I'd been getting itchy feet, knew that the holidays were coming up and, to be honest, I thought that kind of care work would be fairly light compared to what I had been doing. I didn't think I would have to get very emotionally invested. Up to a point, I was right.'

'But?'

'But that just isn't how I function. Don't get me wrong, there are some absolutely wonderful childcare workers there, and they are doing a brilliant job, but it's not for me. The work seems to be more . . . I don't know, more about *containment*. There is *definitely* therapeutic work being done; I just don't think that I've been doing any of it.'

'So you're still uncertain as to what you want to do?'

'Yes.'

'I called you because a temporary post has just become available. It may continue and become longer term, I don't know yet. In many ways, that will depend on you.'

'You want to see how I perform?'

16

'You could say that. Or another way of putting it may be that I want to see if you like it and want to stay.'

'Well, which is it?'

He laughed and crushed the butt. 'Both and neither. One of my staff is leaving. She's pregnant. The children we work with are often quite physical. I won't have her putting herself or her baby at risk, so I have insisted that she remain desk-based until she's ready to take her maternity leave. We have some programmes that could do with further development, and I've set her to work on that. You're more than qualified for her job; you have plenty of experience and I know we can get along. This project is run under the auspices of a voluntary organization set up by a wealthy Irish-American, a Mrs Dunleavy. She left a generous sum of money when she died and wished it to be spent on the care of children in the city of her birth. Her executors set up this project. We work closely with the Health Executive, the ISPCC, the Department of Justice and countless other organizations involved in childcare and child protection.

'Our job is fairly simple. When a child reaches a point where, for any combination of reasons, they have exhausted the resources of the available support services and are to be placed in a secure institution, we are called in. We work with children in mainstream residential care, on foster placement, and those who are still living at home with their parents, but they all have one thing in common: they are in severe crisis and have become unmanageable to their primary carers. Through therapeutic means, we strive to resolve those crises and restore order and good relations between the children and the adults who care for them, whether those adults be parents or care staff.'

'Jane mentioned that you work primarily with children with special needs?'

Ben nodded and smiled. 'Indeed. The children we work with all have special needs. They've been through special schools, some have experienced a variety of foster homes and one child on our books was left on the steps of a church as an infant. He has never known anything *but* being in care. If you were to look through the files on these kids, you would see labels like "attention deficit hyper-activity disorder", "Asperger's syndrome", "intellectual disability", "challenging behaviour", "childhood schizophrenia", and I'm only scratching the surface. What it breaks down to is this: the children who are sent to me don't fit in anywhere else. They've been diagnosed with a range of disorders, some clinical, some purely psychological, and they all exhibit an array of behavioural problems that make them unsuitable for mainstream care. This is a house of last resort. If we can't help, it's a secure institution: a high-support unit, a juvenile lock-up, a psychiatric hospital.'

'The house of last resort. So there's no pressure on the staff then.'

'Ella – the lady you will be filling in for, if you decide to come on board – calls this "Last Ditch House". It's probably as good a name as any.'

'What are the hours?'

'This is the voluntary sector, so they aren't nine-to-five. You're expected to clock up thirty-nine hours a week, but they can be at any time. I *will* ask you to do some evening work and you'll have to work the occasional weekend.'

'That's okay. I'm used to it. The caseload?'

'Because of the nature of the cases, it'll be quite small, no more than three at a time. The work is intensive and short term. You'd see your clients daily for up to maybe a couple of months. If you hadn't effected change by then, we'd either try a different worker, or accept that we couldn't do anything and step aside.'

'Salary?'

'Standard childcare rates. We're linked to residential. Team Leader scale.'

A Team Leader is kind of a middle-manager in a residential childcare setting. A basic salary at this level is around €48,000 per annum.

I was both intrigued and horrified. Ben seemed once again to read my mind.

'It's nothing if not interesting. You won't be bored, I'll tell you that. Are you in?'

I stood up.

'I'm going to have to think about it. Can I ring you in a couple of hours?'

He stood up and shook my hand.

'Let me know by five this evening. You need to be sure this is right for you. But just remember: *I want you on board*. I know what happened in your last job. You did nothing wrong, and you responded to a very difficult set of circumstances in the only way you could have. I've spoken to Jane about how you've done at the unit, too. The doubts you're experiencing are *normal*. We all go through them from time to time.'

He squeezed my hand and smiled.

'I look forward to hearing from you. I know you'll make the right decision.'

I left my car where it was parked and walked.

The heat from the summer sun seeped through the back of my shirt and within fifteen minutes I had worked up a good sweat, although I was not going very fast. I was not headed anywhere in particular. The business sector gave way to residential neighbourhoods with mature gardens, where men watered their lawns and children played on brightly coloured plastic slides and in inflatable paddling pools. An hour later I was beyond this prosperous area and on the side of the dual carriageway, heading south. I was peripherally aware that in five or six miles I could loop back around and into the city centre again.

I walked and I thought. Somewhere around four o'clock that afternoon, worn out and no closer to knowing what to do, I sat down at a small bar called Moynihan's, near where I lived. The landlord, who knew me as a regular, judged from my demeanour that I was not looking for conversation and simply pulled me a pint without having to be asked.

Besides the proprietor, the pub was empty. I sat and stared into space. Did I want to get involved in the kind of work Ben was proposing? Teaching was honourable, had its own challenges and allowed me generous holidays to experiment with childcare for a bit longer until I was really sure. There was a lot to be said for that. So why then did I feel so drawn back to the work? Why did I feel that I had somehow sold out by running away from it?

Why did I have a hole inside me which I knew would not be filled until I had a caseload? I sipped the Guinness and felt it slide down my throat, cold, bitter and delicious.

All Ben was suggesting was a two-month contract, which would take me up to the end of the summer holidays anyway. If it was going well, I could stay – if Ben would have me. If I felt I was out of my depth, I could simply call it a day and go back to the college. Ben had, with his usual forethought, left me with an escape route, one that could be navigated with no loss of face. I downed the pint in two deep gulps. I motioned for the landlord to draw me another, and went over to the old pay-phone in the corner.

Ben did not beat around the bush.

'Well?'

'Before I answer you,' I said, 'I have a question.'

'Of course. Ask what you will.'

'What is the success rate?'

'I beg your pardon?'

'You told me earlier that the work was always based around brief, intensive bursts of therapy, and that if these were not successful, you stepped aside and accepted that you couldn't effect change. What's the success rate? How often do you *not* have to step aside?'

'Ahhh.'

The line went silent.

'You still there?'

'Yes, yes. My, Shane, you do ask awkward questions. Don't you know after all this time that success is hard to measure in this line of work?'

'Ben, you're avoiding the issue. How often do the

children remain in their homes and, more to the point, how many end up in those secure institutions we're trying to keep them out of?'

'If your decision will be based on my answer, perhaps I can save both of us the trouble and withdraw my offer.'

'It's an honest question, asked purely out of professional interest. I deserve to know what I'm getting myself into.'

'Does that mean you're in?'

'Looks like it does.'

'Can you start tomorrow? I've got your cases all lined up.'

'I'll see you at nine. I still want an answer, though, Ben.'

'I haven't worked out a statistic, but I'd say we succeed about as often as we fail. It's about "even-Steven". Sorry I can't give you a more encouraging figure.'

'That's about what I thought. I have a pint waiting for me. See you in the morning. Have the coffee on.'

'You've made the right choice, Shane. Welcome to Last Ditch House.'

2

The following morning, Ben *had* the coffee on. He had, in fact, gone one better and ordered in some freshly baked breads. The offices smelt like a *boulangerie*. A small meeting room had been set up for the team, and we convened briefly before the working day began.

The team was a small one. Besides Ben, four other workers sat around the table: two male, two female. Marian was about my own age, stockily built with short blonde hair and a quiet, thoughtful manner. Loretta was slightly older – I put her in her early forties. She was short, with a smiling, open face, dressed in a mannish way with a flat-top haircut left long at the back. Jerome was tall and gangly, clean-shaven and dressed in denim. Clive was a thick-set man with a confident manner and a ready wit, able to fill any gap in the conversation. I liked them all immediately, and was struck by Ben's ability to form such a cohesive, fluidly functioning group.

The team members gave a short run-down of their cases and how they were doing with them. I listened intently. When Clive, the last of the four, had given his report, and each person had made some short comments on what he had said, Ben pulled over a grey folder.

'I've allocated Shane three cases from the list of new referrals we discussed last week, based on the ranking we gave them. Shane will be working, initially at least, with the Walsh family, the Henrys and the Byrne children.'

The names were greeted with murmurs of recognition and much nodding.

'Okay. We'll all meet in a fortnight to discuss our progress,' Ben said. 'Let's go to work.'

I stayed where I was, as did Ben, the folder still open before him on the desk. I refilled our coffee mugs and pushed my smokes towards him.

'So, where is my first port of call?'

'I'd like you to visit the Walshes this morning,' Ben said, leafing through one of the files in the folder. 'Interesting case. Two little boys: Bobby, aged six, Micky, aged four. Their mother, Biddy, is a widow. They live out in Haroldstown.'

'Gangland.'

'Yes. The father, Toddy, was killed in a shooting two years ago. He was well known to the police, and it came as no surprise. There has been steady social-work involvement – they were in there even before Mr Walsh met his untimely demise. Pre-school teachers reported fears of physical neglect, and there were concerns about *emotional* neglect after the death. Mrs Walsh seemed to find it very hard to cope.'

'Okay, how does this involve us, though? It sounds like the kind of stuff that would stay on the Health Executive's books for years.'

Ben pulled on his cigarette and nodded vigorously. 'Agreed. What sets this one apart is a rather peculiar little detail. Six months ago, Bobby informed his class at the daily news session that his daddy had come back. His teacher assumed that he meant Biddy had taken up with a new man, so she put little or no pass on it. However, it became clear that this was not the case. Micky had made similar comments at pre-school. They were indicating that Toddy Walsh had returned.'

'From the dead?'

'Yes. The social worker on the case spoke to both children at length about it. It seems the two boys often go to play down the bottom of their garden, and when they do, every day, from what they have said, their father appears to them. They both see him and speak with him.'

'Does the mother see him too?'

'No, but she hasn't gone out of her way to discourage the fantasy. She seems to be buying into it, finding comfort in it almost.'

'I take it that Mrs Walsh is still grieving?'

'Very much so. She has most certainly *not* moved on.'

'It's not an unusual childhood fantasy though, is it? I mean, it's simply a form of imaginary friend.'

'I'd tend to lean that way myself, except that the boys' behaviour has become increasingly erratic and violent since the alleged visitations began. The social worker was unsuccessful in breaking the pattern of behaviour. A therapist from child psychiatry made a few visits, and reports that, rather than this being simply a case of, as you so reasonably say, imaginary friends, the boys are having visual and auditory hallucinations. They have had to be removed from school because of their outbursts of violence. Biddy is now saying that she cannot manage them. They have even had to be kept inside the house and garden because of their attacks on local children.'

'And this all began when they started seeing their father? There was no aggression before that?'

'No. The boys say that he is actually *telling* them to behave in this way. Their behaviour was always reserved before this, according to teachers and neighbours.'

'So we're probably looking at some kind of repressed anger. They need their dead father to give them permission to act out just how devastated they feel at the loss.'

Ben grinned. 'That seems a good place to begin. But use it as a starting point, no more than that. I want you to do some simple play work with these boys, and see what comes out. Who knows, we might all be surprised.'

Haroldstown was five square miles of housing estates built like a patchwork quilt on the north side of the city, with no particular thought to consistency of architectural style or even to quality of building materials. Some of the houses were constructed to last: solid, angular blocks of stone work, created in the late nineteen fifties and still standing firm and strong, while others were more elaborate, wooden-framed concoctions that had degenerated into crumbling wreckages within a bare five years, seeming to have been moulded from papier-mâché. The vast majority of the structures were built by the local authority, and, while not nearly as devoid of redemption as the Oldtown flats, the area had long been run by a series of criminal gangs. These groups operated pretty much in full view of everyone, including the police. Ask any family in Haroldstown and they could tell you who was the leader of the Northside Bandits, or the Haroldstown Tribe. The gangs were given these lurid titles by the tabloids, and their commanders were all christened with similar nick-names – the Captain, the Rottweiler, the Accountant. It made you feel as if the whole thing was part of the sixties' *Batman* TV show.

The problem was that this was real, and, as easy as it was to poke fun at the inherent silliness of it all, these groups *were* menacing. Execution-style shootings were becoming more and more common. Feuds now ended in deaths on an all too regular basis. Some saw the gangs as the people's way of reacting to the abject poverty they lived in, but that was an overly simplistic analysis of the situation. The gangs may have started out that way, but they had degenerated into a cycle of self-perpetuating violence, and the people they preyed on were not the wealthy or those who had some hope of altering the status quo. Drugs were peddled to young people right there in the estates. Prostitutes were recruited from the scores of young women unable to earn money to feed their fatherless babies. And the bodies that were found in ditches or lying in the gutter, shot at close range in the base of the skull, were all unemployed Haroldstown residents, usually 'known to the police' as active participants in organized crime.

Toddy Walsh had been one of these young men. I remembered the newspaper reports of his death. He had been the equivalent of middle management in one of the ferocious, smaller groups, dubbed by a local journalist as the 'Twilight Posse'. Obviously an ambitious individual, Toddy had attempted to stage a hostile takeover of the Posse's board. The problem was that his supporters were easily swayed from their purpose and he had been sold out. He was found on a patch of wasteland not far from where he lived. He had been shot in the back of the head at point-blank range with a heavy-gauge shotgun, but not before he had been tortured viciously. The Gardaí had to identify him from his dental records.

The Walshes lived on a narrow street deep in the heart of Haroldstown. Each side of the road was lined with terraced houses, pressed upon each other as if they were seeking comfort or warmth. I parked up on the cracked footpath outside the tiny, overgrown garden of the Walsh residence. Women, still clad in dressing gowns at ten thirty in the morning, were standing at their gates chatting. They stared at the strange car and the unknown man arriving outside the hard-luck house. What further misery was being brought upon this sad little family? A dozen eyes followed me up the short pathway to the warped front door. I knocked smartly and waited, ignoring the accusing eyes and mutters.

Biddy Walsh looked like someone who'd had every last vestige of joy wrung from her. A tall, thin woman with stringy black hair and hollow, pockmarked cheeks, she had probably once been very attractive. Now she carried the shadow of her pain around like the walking wounded. She looked me over with resentment, coupled with what seemed to be almost relief. I could tell that she was close to breaking point and was well aware that she needed help, but that a redundant sense of etiquette would stop her from giving me too much information. Like it or not, I represented everything that had kept her people, the population of this ghetto, subjugated for so long. I was

The Man, or at least his cipher, and therefore not to be cooperated with.

I introduced myself.

She said nothing. I waited for what seemed like a polite amount of time and then cleared my throat.

'Er, can I come in, Mrs Walsh? If I'm to do some work with Bobby and Micky, I'll have to be able to see them, won't I?'

She stepped aside and allowed me in, but her eyes were full of suspicion and anxiety. The hallway was dark and gloomy and a stale smell of cooking hung in the air, even though it was only ten thirty, and I doubted very much that she had been cooking since the evening before: fried breakfasts were a luxury few in Haroldstown could afford. The walls in the hallway were covered with photographs of Biddy and her family, but I was not invited to stop and admire them. Still unspeaking, she brushed past me through a door to my left. I followed.

The living room was moderately better lit but would still be difficult to read in. The curtains were only partially open, and a sheen of dirt coated the windowpane. Biddy sat on a grimy couch and stared into space. I looked about and saw an armchair covered in unironed clothes. I picked them up, made as neat a pile of them as I could and placed them on a coffee table. Then I sat down. The walls of this room were also completely hidden by framed photographs – hundreds of them, in fact. I could see Biddy in some of them, looking young and happy, beside a dark-haired, dark-eyed man who was looking into the camera with a steely gaze. He was not handsome: there was something cruel about the set of his mouth, and his eyebrows met in the middle, but he certainly looked striking. This, I assumed, was Toddy Walsh. As my eyes travelled around the countless images, I saw that he was in almost every single photograph. With him and Biddy in some of the snapshots were two little boys. I could trace them through infancy and into early childhood. The boys were both dark, like their parents, although the older one seemed to resemble his father more, while the younger mostly took after the mother.

'Where are the boys, Mrs Walsh?'

Slowly, she turned to look at me.

'They're with him.'

'I'm sorry . . .'

'They're out the back with their father.'

A sense of dread washed over me. I pushed the feeling aside and smiled.

'Great! Well, that's perfect. Can I go out and meet them? It would be great to see exactly what they're doing. It's a good place to start actually.'

A look of horror spread across her face at the prospect.

'No! No, you stay here and I'll go and get them, bring them to you!'

'I'd like to go to them . . .' I pressed, sensing this was a sore point, but wanting to see where it would lead.

'No! I said no.'

She stood up, trembling now. As she walked to the door, I called after her: 'Mrs Walsh, can I ask you why you don't want me to go out to the boys?'

She stopped with her back to me, her head lowered.

'Because,' she said, her voice a whisper, 'you'll frighten him off. I want the boys to get better, not to be so wild.

They're being eaten up by what's happening – they don't understand it. I'm terrible worried about them, so I am. The social workers tell me you can cure them. I want you to do that for me. For *them*. Give them peace. But you're not to drive him away. Not now that he's come back to us.'

Then she was gone. I sat for some minutes, considering what had just passed between us. There was a lot I still didn't understand, so I decided to simply focus on the boys for the time being.

I stood up and opened the curtains to better let the daylight in and then went back out to my car and got a box of tissues. I cleaned the window as best I could. When I was finished, the room, while far from pleasant, was reasonably bright. It was a start. I then brought in a box, from the boot of my car, which contained a few simple toys and some felt-tip pens and paper.

Five or six minutes later, Biddy came in with the two boys. I felt like I knew them already, even though it was only from the countless pictures that were all around me. Bobby was six years old and taller by a head than his brother. Size aside, they were very similar, except that Bobby had the hard, adversarial gaze and firmly set mouth of his father, while Micky retained the melancholic, gentler visage of his mother. They stood in the doorway of the room, side by side, watching me with exactly the same trepidation and worry their mother had displayed on my arrival. I had the toys (mostly cars and figurines) and drawing equipment spread out on the floor before me.

'Boys, I'm glad to meet you. Come on over and let's have a chat.'

The children did not move, but Biddy gently pushed them towards me. Obediently they moved forward and stood in front of me. I smiled at them and motioned for them to sit. I was already cross-legged on the floor. Bobby threw a look over his shoulder at his mother and, when she nodded, lowered himself to the carpet, followed by Micky.

'You can leave us, Mrs Walsh. Keep the door open, please. I'll give you a shout when I'm done.'

She left. I looked at the two boys.

'Well, lads. I'm Shane. You've met some other people, haven't you, who've come to chat with you since you've started having some problems at school and whatnot?'

The boys listened, wide-eyed. Micky gave a slight nod.

'I'm not really here to talk. I'm going to be meeting you every day for the next few weeks, just to play. We'll have one hour every day at this time, and in that hour you can do whatever you like. It's your time. I've brought some toys and games with me, as you can see, but we can use your toys too, if you want. We can play in here or in the garden; it's completely up to you. This is your special time, and my job is just to be here and make sure you have the best time you can.'

The boys looked at me, still keeping whatever they were thinking or feeling to themselves, although I could see Micky eyeing the toys longingly.

'So what do you want to do today? I thought you might like to play with the cars and trucks and things, or maybe we could do some colouring and drawing? It's up to you.'

I did not want to prompt them any more than that. I stopped talking and watched. There was a great deal of communication going on between them, but it was all non-verbal. Micky, with his eyes, was imploring his older brother to give it a go, but Bobby was staunchly refusing, remaining po-faced and impassive. Micky reached out a hand and tugged his brother's sleeve. The gesture was met by a very slight shake of the head. Micky sighed in exasperation and seemed to decide to take the situation into his own hands. On his butt, he scooted over to the toys and picked up a yellow truck. Casting occasional looks at his brother, who was observing him in disbelief and disapproval, he began to examine the vehicle. After a brief once-over, Micky started to push it on a winding path in and out of the other toys I had laid out on the floor, making a loud engine noise to accompany its progress. Bobby could not stand this mutinous behaviour any longer.

'Micky, you shouldn'a done that! We said we wouldn' talk to these peoples no more! They wants to take us away from Mam.'

'I din' talk to him, Bob. Looka the toys he's bringed. None o' the others bringed us toys. He said he doesn' *want* to talk, anyway. All we gots to do is play. Come on. You take the digger!'

Bobby was jiggling up and down on his haunches at this stage, obviously really wanting to get involved in his brother's game but feeling that he shouldn't. Micky seemed to be enjoying his brother's discomfort, and pushed the truck over so that it rolled right past Bobby's feet. This was too much for the older boy, and he too scooched over and picked up the digger. The game was afoot.

For this first session I simply sat back and made very little comment about what the boys were doing. 'Play work' is about using children's play as a kind of psychoanalytical experience, so the play-worker will record what has occurred and will then try to analyse any patterns or particular symbols that emerge. I did not want the boys to see me writing down anything, so I made mental notes, but to be honest it would take more than one session for any recurring patterns to evolve.

The play on that first day was rudimentary. The boys cleared a space on the floor, lined up some of the cars and trucks and made an imaginary building site, taking turns with each of the vehicles. The digger was used to make pretend holes and fill them in, so I suppose I could have posited that the boys were trying to 'bury' their feelings about the loss of their father, but that seemed too trite. They ignored me once the game began, and I was glad of that. It meant that I could sit back without interruption and observe. The dynamic between them was interesting. It had seemed at first that Bobby was in charge, but Micky had taken the lead and initiated the play. As the game continued, the boys took turns being leader, and it was simply impossible to discern who was the alpha male between them. They were both strong personalities, and they appeared to accept instinctively that each had character strengths that sometimes had to be brought to the fore. It was a surprisingly mature relationship for children of such young ages, but then, I mused, they had been neglected since their father's death, left largely to their own devices. They had grown up much more quickly than many children.

With ten minutes remaining before the session was to finish, I interrupted the game. There was something I wanted to try.

'Boys, I'd like you to draw something for me. Is that okay?'

Micky clapped his hands and laughed. 'Yeah, sure! I'm a good drawer, I am. I always keep the colours between the lines. Don't I, Bob?'

Bobby nodded and took the page I pushed across to him. I ripped open the package of felt-tip pens and handed them over.

'Now. When I got here, you were both down the bottom of the garden, weren't you?'

They nodded.

'What were you doing?'

'We were down talking with our daddy.'

There it was. As simple and open as that.

'Right. I want you both to draw your daddy for me. What does he look like? Try and remember for me what he was like just now, when you were with him.'

Fantasies like the one the boys were experiencing are often purely instinctive, an almost automatic response to a crisis. Making them put down on paper what they were seeing could be enough to cause the delusion to end. After all, they weren't *really* seeing anything.

The boys looked at me with wide eyes, but nodded

and grabbed the markers. They put their heads together, bending low over the pages on the floor. Another thought occurred to me.

'Hey, how's about we have a competition? Shall we see who can draw the better picture?'

I don't usually encourage competitiveness in play situations, but I had an ulterior motive in this instance.

'Bobby, why don't you go over there, and Micky, you go over there.'

I put them at opposite ends of the room.

'Now, when I say go, you both start drawing, and when I say stop, you have to stop, and bring the pictures over to me here, and we'll see which is the best.'

'I'll win, I'll win!' Micky chanted, bouncing up and down.

'Will not!' Bobby retorted. 'My teacher always told me I was a great drawer! I'll win!'

'Well, we'll have to see,' I said. 'Ready, set . . . go!'

Both heads immediately went down and furious scribbling began. Five minutes later, Bobby looked over at me through slitted eyes.

'What's the prize for this?'

I grinned. 'You just wait and see. It's a good one.'

A shrug was my only response and the busy activity continued. After they had been drawing for ten minutes, I called time.

'That's it! Bring 'em over here and let's have a look.'

Both boys bounded over, slapping the pictures down in my lap, eager looks on their faces. I laughed despite myself. No matter how tough the situation, no matter how disturbed the mind or emotions, children are still children.

I turned the pictures so that I could examine what they had drawn, and felt myself suddenly become very cold. I had not expected what I found. In fact, I was not sure what I had expected, but certainly not this.

Both pictures were almost identical, drawn in dark, shadowy colours. The margins were full of swirling, cloud-like shapes, which I knew from my studies of art-therapy were called *vortexes*, and which usually symbolized emotional turmoil. The centre of each page contained a large, terrifying face, simply drawn, yet very clear:

I was reminded of the heads on Easter Island, or of Edvard Munch's *The Scream*. The image in the drawings was not of something pleasant or loving, not of a father whom the boys loved and revered. It bore no resemblance to the countless pictures on the walls around us. What was so hard to understand and was impossible to explain was that, independently, *both boys had drawn exactly the same thing*. They stood before me grinning, both obviously very proud of their efforts.

'So?' Micky said, pointing at the pictures. 'Who wins?'

I suddenly became aware that I had broken into a cold sweat and that the room had begun to feel close. I forced myself to smile.

'Lads, they're both too good to choose between. I mean, look at them, they're so alike. You're *both* brilliant artists. Can I keep these pictures?'

Vigorous nodding.

'Well, there's two bits to the prize. First, you get to keep the markers.'

'Cool!'

'Deadly!'

'And . . .' I produced a couple of sugar-free, politically correct lollipops from my pocket. These were met with exclamations of approval. I smiled and told them they could go and play now, because I had finished for today. They ran from the room, lollipop sticks protruding from their mouths.

'Careful you don't fall with those in your mouths; you'll choke yourselves,' I called after them, knowing I was wasting my time.

I looked again at the two drawings of the thing the boys believed to be their father. I folded the pictures and put them in the box with the toys. I had to admit, I was at a loss. I wandered out to the kitchen, where Mrs Walsh was sitting at the table, a cup of tea in front of her. I looked out the grimy window at the garden, where these two little boys communed with something, real or imagined, that looked like a creature from a primeval nightmare.

'So,' Biddy's voice drifted up to me, 'will we be seeing you again?'

'Yes. I'll see you tomorrow.'

'Can you do anything for my boys?'

I continued to gaze at the ditch at the end of the narrow garden.

'I really don't know, Mrs Walsh, but I'm sure as hell going to try.'

Biddy released a deep sigh, as if from her very core.

'Well, at least you're honest.'

'Let's hope I've got a bit more than that going for me.'

'Mister, it's a good start.'

3

Garibaldi Street smelt of money.

Georgian town houses, dripping affluence, lined each side of the wide road, the cars in the driveways costing double what most of the dwellings in Haroldstown were worth. If I had been an estate agent, I would have used words like 'secluded', 'exclusive' and 'well established' about the street. But I wasn't an estate agent, and what I saw around me as I looked for the home of the Henry family left me cold. Garibaldi Street was about living as performance art. You don't often see topiary any more, but more than one of the houses looked as if they had employed Edward Scissorhands to maintain their hedges. The cars seemed to never have been driven; they adorned the driveways like ornaments, waxed to within an inch of their lives: BMWs, Audis, Mercs ... and since this was a work-day, I had to assume that these were second cars. I was driving a 1981 Austin Allegro, and, as I pulled it over to the curb outside the address I'd been given for Molly and Dirk Henry, I didn't bother to reach for the wheel-lock. The only way my car would be stolen in this neighbourhood would be as a practical joke.

Molly Henry opened the door, a tall, heavily made-up woman in her early forties. She was dressed in a linen pant-suit and had a pashmina draped awkwardly over her shoulders, despite the heat of the day; I reckoned that the woman at the store had told her that it 'completed the outfit'. I wondered if it were pinned somewhere to keep it from falling off.

'Mr Dunphy, thank you so much for coming out to see us.'

I took her hand, which she left resting on my own limply for a second or two before pulling it back. It wasn't a handshake, more a gesture of contact.

'Come in, please. Dirk is on the veranda.'

The inside of the house was as I would have expected it to be. Deep pile carpets, plaster busts, wallpaper just the right side of garish, art hanging here and there which didn't look like prints, but matched the colour scheme perfectly. I assumed that they redecorated seasonally.

I was shown through to a patio out the back, over-looking a spacious garden that contained more topiary and a complex system of ponds, streams and waterfalls. All the while I was looking for some evidence of the child whom I knew was around and about somewhere. What I was seeing was like a show-house designed by a Stepford Wife. If there was a child here, she had to be locked up in the basement.

Dirk was tanned and slim and looked as if he had more money than the Hiltons. He stood to meet me, and his handshake was firm and manly. He looked slightly younger than his wife, and I noticed him giving my decidedly unorthodox appearance a once-over. This was, however, followed by what seemed to be an internal shrug, as if to say – 'these guys are all hippies anyway'; he would give me a chance, see what I could do. He had a jug of lemonade and three glasses filled with ice on the table before him, and he motioned me to sit. Without asking, he poured the drinks.

'Mr Dunphy, I'm delighted that you've taken the trouble to come all the way out here to see us.' His voice was rich and resonant, like a newsreader's. 'I don't imagine you have much call to come to this part of town.'

'Not a lot. And call me Shane. We'll be seeing a lot of each other, for a couple of weeks at least. It would be easier if we drop the formalities.'

He grinned, displaying perfect teeth.

'Of course, Shane. I'm Dirk, and this is Molly.'

His wife simpered and nodded at me.

'So,' I said, taking a sip of the lemonade – it was delicious, and in the thick summer heat very welcome – 'why have you asked to see someone from the Dunleavy Trust?'

'Well, I did give all the relevant information to Mr Tyrrell.'

'I apologize, Dirk. This is my first day. I have only had a cursory glance at your file. I'd prefer to hear it from you anyway.'

'Very well.' Dirk Henry adjusted himself on his seat. 'Molly and I have a daughter, Mina. She is seventeen. For the past year, Mina has been running away, on an almost monthly basis. She disappears from her room, and often we may not see her until the following day. She returns, refuses to tell us where she has been, and simply goes up to her room again. It is most worrying.'

I nodded and rubbed my beard.

'I don't want to make little of this – it's obviously quite

42

distressing for you both – but has she got any friends she might be going to? Have you rung around?'

'There is no one she would go to who would not inform us immediately of her arrival. You see, Shane, our daughter is special.'

I looked at the couple blankly.

'All children are special, Dirk.'

'You misunderstand me. She has Down's Syndrome.'

'Oh.'

I felt like kicking myself for not taking longer over the file. A seventeen-year-old girl roaming the streets of the city at night was ripe for exploitation, but a teenager with Down's Syndrome was even more at risk. Her parents had every reason to be worried.

'Well, let's look at it from a practical point of view,' I said, setting down my glass. 'This may seem obvious, but have you tried asking her where she's going?'

'Of course,' Dirk said, reaching into his shirt pocket and producing a box of cigars. 'She simply goes silent. I know that the accepted wisdom about Down's is that sufferers are intellectually subnormal, but in many ways Mina is very bright. She can be quite articulate when the mood takes her, but she can also clam up and play stupid too. When the topic of her disappearances is brought up, she simply smiles sweetly and shuts down. She has not given us a single word of explanation.'

I nodded. Dirk offered me a cigar, but I refused. It was too hot for such a heavy smoke.

'You must have some suspicion about where she's going. What does your gut tell you?'

'We're at a complete loss, Shane. I simply can't begin to think of where she's going or what she's doing.'

I looked over at the demure Molly. 'Women's intuition, Molly? What do you think she's up to?'

She smiled and wrung her hands. 'I'm afraid I must concur with my husband. I have no idea what Mina is up to.'

I sighed and turned back to Dirk. I didn't believe Molly. Something in her tone, in her body-language, told me that she *did* know, or at least suspected, what Mina's exploits were about, but I let it slide. A major confrontation at this stage of our relationship would likely do more harm than good.

'Have you checked to see if there's a pattern to her disappearances? Does it always happen at the same time? Is there anything in her life that triggers the action? Could it be a lunar thing? I know that may sound bizarre, but I've worked in places where extra staff are called in at every full moon. The moon can affect some people very strongly.'

'No,' Dirk said. 'There is no obvious pattern to her movements. I worked for a time in Human Resources, so I'm familiar with the theory you have mentioned. I don't believe that Mina is being upset by the lunar cycle.'

'Is it possible she's being coerced into going out? Is there anyone outside the family who has an undue influence over her?'

'Not that we're aware of. We are in close contact with the staff and management of the workshop she attends during the day. They tell us that Mina is very happy and content, and she certainly seems to have only good things to say about it to us. We know all the young people she associates with – we meet them at the youth club she attends every week. There is no one among them who would wish her harm or would put her at risk.'

I sat back and considered this. There was one final set of questions that needed to be asked, but I was loath to bring them up. I knew from experience that they often caused alarm. There was, however, nothing to be done but to get it over with. I took a deep breath.

'What about the staff at either the workshop or the club? I hate to be negative, but some people are attracted to this type of work specifically to gain access to vulnerable people. Is there anyone – any *adult* – who has taken an unusual interest in Mina over the past year? What are the screening procedures at the club? For voluntary endeavours like youth clubs, they tend to be rather lax.'

As I expected, the Henrys became visibly paler. Dirk cleared his throat and tried to force a smile.

'I suppose we have considered such a possibility, but we abandoned it. All the adults, volunteers and professionals alike, have only the best interests of the client group at heart. I do not believe for a moment that there's anything sinister afoot.'

'Dirk,' I said as gently as I could, 'you are being naive. There will always be people involved in the caring professions for less than honourable reasons. Now, with a bit of luck, that is not the case here, but that doesn't mean that it isn't worth investigating. I'll check out what the procedure is for the workshop. I'd imagine that it's the standard Garda clearance check – which is far from foolproof, by the way. As for this youth club, the fact of the matter is that there probably isn't any checking done at all. That means that anyone can walk in off the street and have access to all those young people.'

'Oh God,' Molly gasped, her hand to her mouth.

'Now I'm not trying to alarm you, but it has to be something we consider.'

'I understand your drawing our attention to this, Shane,' Dirk said, a steely tone entering into his voice at the sight of his wife's distress, 'but I stand over my previous assertion – I do not believe that this avenue of investigation will come to anything.'

'I sincerely hope not,' I said.

This was getting me nowhere fast. These were intelligent people. It seemed that they had exhausted most reasonable options in trying to redress the situation. There was little left for me to do without meeting Mina.

'Well, it seems to me that the most sensible thing to do is to focus on issues of safety. You have to ensure that she doesn't *get* out, at the very least until we can find out where she's going. I'm guessing you have a fairly complex security system in the house?'

'Of course.'

'Does Mina know how to get around it? Does she know how to disable the system, key-codes, that sort of thing?'

'We don't think so, although she is quite observant . . . no, I'm sure she doesn't know how to shut down the system.'

'Have you used it to try and contain her before?'

'Well, not really. It seemed a bit draconian. We put

bolts on the windows, a latch on the front door, that kind of thing.'

'But it didn't work?'

'No.'

'Possibly it's time to try something different then.'

They looked embarrassed.

'You both need to be committed to this. If it's going to work, if we are going to keep your daughter safe, then you must be firm. Tough love. If not, well I cannot guarantee that we'll make any progress.'

Dirk puffed on his cigar and tapped some ash onto the cobbles of the patio.

'We understand that. If we can't stop this wanderlust she seems to have developed, we are aware that she will have to be institutionalized. I do not want that for my daughter. There is something going on with her that I don't understand, but I *want* to understand it. I want to help her. I *know* that we can sort this out. If she's unhappy, then let's try and make her happy again. If she needs something she's not getting at home, let's find out what it is and see if we can't get it for her. If she's lonely, let's help her make some new friends. I love my daughter, Mr Dunphy. Help me to help her.'

Without looking, he reached out his hand and Molly took it.

'I'm not promising anything, Dirk, but I will do my best. Can I see her?'

Dirk checked his watch. 'She'll be home shortly. She's at the workshop, but she should be on her way.'

'No problem. I'll wait.'

Ten minutes later, the doorbell rang.

'That'll be her escort now,' Dirk said. People with special needs, when travelling to and from school or work, are often accompanied on the bus by an escort, to ensure their safety while in transit. The escort will see them safely to their front door, ensure their parents are there to meet them, and then head on to the next stop. It may seem unnecessary, but there are many people with special needs who have epilepsy, or who suffer from behavioural problems, and the driver can't steer the bus and cope with a *grand mal* seizure at the same time.

Molly shot out of her chair and returned with a tall, dark-haired girl with the obvious facial characteristics of Down's Syndrome. Down's is a genetic condition, caused by an extra chromosome on the twenty-first pair. You often see it referred to as *Trisomy Twenty-One*. Individuals born with Down's Syndrome usually carry certain identifiable physical traits: almond-shaped eyes, a smaller mouth cavity, which causes the appearance of an outsized tongue, a stocky, short build, malformation of the fingers (technically called *polydactyly*) and smaller than normal ears. They usually face a range of challenges, not the least of which is the set of preconceived notions society has about them.

Down's Syndrome is the flagship 'special need'. Look at the adverts for the Special Olympics when it comes around. You'll see that every ad depicts a person with Down's. This is because they are easily recognizable, tend to be seen as 'cute' and because their facial features make it look as if they are always smiling. People with Down's Syndrome are believed to be fun-loving, physically affectionate, saintly in disposition, sweet and gentle. The truth is that individuals with Down's Syndrome are just the same as anyone else. They are people, and no set of beliefs or social norms can sum them up. They are all individuals.

Down's Syndrome, as Dirk had already mentioned, is also associated with intellectual disability, usually within the 'mild' spectrum (meaning an IQ of between 60 and 75, or a mental age of between five and seven years). This is also a ridiculously simplistic view. Young people with Down's Syndrome now regularly pass the Leaving Certificate (the Irish equivalent of A levels) and adults with Down's or comparable 'disorders' hold down a range of jobs and contribute to their communities in many positive ways.

Mina did not have the short, stocky build that is common, but her facial features were clearly pronounced. She was dressed fashionably and her dark hair was long, rich and thick, expensively styled and with blonde highlights. I stood when she came over to the table, holding out my hand. She seemed to take more after her father than her mother and her grip was firm when she shook hands.

'Very pleased to meet you,' she said as her father introduced us.

The smaller mouth cavity often causes speech impediments of varying degrees, and Mina was no different. Her speech was slurred, with a pronounced lisping of the sibilants. I could, however, understand her well enough as long as I listened carefully.

'Mina, do you know why I'm here?' I asked.

She nodded. 'I think so, yes.'

'And . . .'

'Mum and Dad want you to get me under control.'

'Now Mina –' Dirk started, but I held up my hand and he stopped. It probably would have been better to have talked to her without her parents present, but I needed her to get used to me first. I didn't want to frighten her.

'Would you say your behaviour has been out of control?'

She smiled at me. She was a pretty kid, and I bet that smile had got her out of a lot of trouble over the years. I'll admit, I did feel myself warming to her. There was a real strength of character here, but also an iron will that was not easily going to yield to enforced boundaries.

'No, I *don't* think I'm out of control.'

'Well, I can see you and your parents disagree on that point, so let's move on to something else. Tell me about yourself.'

'What would you like to know?'

'Well, you're in the workshop. How's that going for you?'

'I like it well enough. I have some good friends there.'

'Do you look forward to going to work every day?'

'Not always. Do *you* look forward to going to work every day?'

'Not always,' I smiled. 'Tell me about your friends. What are they like?'

'I'm not sure what you mean. They're like people. Are you asking me if they are retarded like me?'

I felt the word like a slap in the face. She had come

out with it so fast that I was totally unprepared, and it made me doubt myself. Is that what I *had* meant? No, I decided, it wasn't. I had actually been trying to assess whether or not Mina was lonely and if that might be the cause of her sudden disappearances. I realized that I had fallen for a standard defensive tactic. Mina knew that she was at fault, and was trying to turn the tables by making me the baddie. I decided to come right back at her, let her see that I would not be easily diverted.

'Mina, you don't know me. When you get to know me, you'll learn that I never use words like that, and also I don't really care about whether or not a person is "normal",' I made inverted commas in the air with my fingers, 'or not. Please don't insult me. I wasn't rude to you.'

She said nothing for a moment, trying to sum me up. I could tell she wasn't used to people being as direct with her as that, and had to think about how to respond. As it happened, she decided to pretend that the little altercation had not occurred.

'I have some good friends in the workshop: people who treat me with respect. There are some people I don't like, and who don't like me. It's just like any other job, I suppose. The staff are nice to us all. Some of them talk to us as if we are real, intelligent people, and I like that very much. There are also staff who treat us all like children. They mean well, but sometimes I still get angry.'

'I can understand that. What do you do when you're not working? Any hobbies, interests?'

'I go to the Abled-Disabled Club on a Tuesday evening.'

'And what's that like?'

'It's a youth club for people with special needs. A lot of the people from the workshop go there.'

'Sounds like fun.'

She shrugged. Maybe it wasn't such fun after all.

'Anything else?'

'I like to listen to my CDs. I watch TV. We go for drives on a Sunday.'

'You and your mum and dad?'

'Yes.'

'Nice. I bet you look forward to that.'

Again the shrug.

'Your mum and dad have been telling me that you've been ... um ... heading off on your own a bit lately. Disappearing. They don't know where you've been going and they're worried about you. Now maybe if they knew where you were going, you could reach some kind of compromise, something that would be agreeable to all of you. So how's about it? Want to tell us what's been going on?'

Mina flashed that smile at me again.

I knew that it was highly unlikely that she would give me an answer. Her parents were sitting there, and she had just met me. But I wanted to see how she would handle the direct approach.

'I don't know what you mean.'

I laughed. 'Don't pull that one on me, Mina. You know perfectly well what I mean. *You* mean that you don't want to talk about it.'

'Yes, but I don't know what you mean.'

'Come on, Mina.'

The smile remained, she stood up and, muttering just like Dustin Hoffman in *Rainman* ('Yeah, I *definitely* don't know what you mean'), wandered back into the house.

Perplexed, I looked at Molly and Dirk.

'Well,' I said, 'that was one hell of a performance.'

Dirk, smiling quietly to himself, nodded. 'Now you see what we've been trying to deal with.'

'We have our work cut out for us,' I agreed.

Dirk laughed and held a match to his cigar, which had gone out.

'Any thoughts on how to proceed?'

I scratched my head and had a sip of lemonade.

'Right now, no. Use the security system at night, so you'll know if she tries to escape. I'll talk to her some more, maybe visit the workshop, see how she is there, pay a visit to this Abled-Disabled Club. Other than that, let's just see what happens.'

'That all sounds a bit vague, Shane,' Molly said.

'Do you think so? I've found in the past that sometimes doing very little is the best course of action. What we need in this instance is for Mina to tell us what's happening. She won't do it in words, so we'll just wait for her to *show* us.'

Dirk and Molly nodded. I actually had no idea whether my plan, or lack of one, would work. Mina was a bright young lady. Something told me that she would not let anything slip intentionally. We would just have to hope she would let down her guard – and do it sooner rather than later.

4

'Rivendell' was a three-storeyed grey stone building that had been a fever hospital during the late Norman era. Set in its own grounds on the east bank of the river, it presented an ominous silhouette in the rapidly descending night. I sat on the bonnet of the Austin and leafed through the last of my case files. I was there to talk to the staff about the Byrne twins.

The house looked as if Norman Bates's mother lived there, and I found it difficult to believe that it was in fact a residential children's home. What kind of thoughts must run through these children's heads, I wondered, as they were brought up the narrow path to this dark, cold, gothic edifice? I shoved the file into my bag, tossed it onto the back seat of the car and walked up the driveway myself. Lights were on in the windows, and bats danced and played around the eaves of the tall parapets, chasing moths and beetles in the dying summer evening. The bats were pipistrelles – small, air-borne mammals that had obviously nested in the attic of the ancient structure. I watched them for a time, finishing a hurried cigarette. Bats don't bother me. They do what they have to do to survive, and do it without malice. If only the same could be said for people.

'Abandon hope all ye who enter here,' I muttered, and rang the doorbell. I heard it echo throughout the halls and stairwells and, after what seemed an age, footsteps clattered in my direction. The door creaked slowly open.

'Shane, is it?'

The person holding open the huge wooden door was perhaps twenty-two years old, with a nose-ring and hair dyed a violent shade of red. She was dressed in a highly appropriate Goth style: all blacks, reds and purples, set off beautifully by a Marilyn Manson T-shirt.

'Yes, I'm from the Dunleavy Trust. I'm here about the Byrnes.'

'Sure, come in, come in. I'm Olwyn, Larry Byrne's key-worker. We're just getting the kids to bed. I'll show you to the staff room, and we'll be with you in a few minutes.'

'Thank you.'

The building smelt like an old convent, residues of incense and candlewax hanging in the air. Olwyn told me, as we walked up two flights of stairs, that it actually had been a convent for almost one hundred years, until the Health Executive had taken it over five years previously, and turned it into a childcare unit. The corridors all had the high ceilings and polished wooden floors of the old institution, the stone walls still lined with paintings of religious scenes: Christ at Cana, turning water into wine; Mary Magdalene, prostrate in the middle of a circle of people hell-bent on having a good stoning, Jesus standing beside her, gazing at the bloodthirsty crowd with stern pity. A crucifix was hanging on the wall above the staff-room door on the third floor, the figure upon it so clearly and realistically rendered in his agony that I had to look away.

'I know,' Olwyn whispered, 'I hate it too. Bríd, the manager, won't get rid of any of that holy stuff. She says it's too valuable.'

'You don't have to burn it,' I whispered back. 'You could just stick it in storage out of the way somewhere. You can't be using *all* these rooms.'

'No. The kids all sleep on the second floor – we've five now, including Larry and Francey. We all live on the ground floor, and we keep the staff room and offices on the top floor here. There's loads of rooms we never even go into. I don't think I've ever seen half of the building. Listen, take a seat, help yourself to a coffee, and I'll be with you in ten minutes or so. Bríd is here and can't wait to meet you, and Karena, Francey's key-worker, has come in especially to meet you. Make yourself comfortable.'

Olwyn's footsteps echoed down the stone stairway.

The staff quarters were comfortably and snugly decorated, with lots of cosy armchairs, racks of magazines (childcare journals, copies of *National Geographic*, women's publications like *Take a Break* and *Woman's Own*, as well as the ubiquitous *Hello!* and *OK!*), a sagging bookshelf, again loaded with a mix of textbooks and novels, a TV and DVD player. A coffee machine with a nearly empty pot sat on a sideboard. I took a mug from a wooden tree. The beverage was not as bad as I had suspected – it obviously hadn't been stewing for too long. I sat down to wait.

Fifteen minutes later Olwyn returned with two other women. She introduced them as Bríd, the manager, and Karena.

In residential, and in some other care settings too,

key-working is a fairly standard practice. It involves one worker taking responsibility for one, or sometimes two, children. This means that the key-worker will attend parent-teacher meetings, shop for Christmas presents for the child, organize dental check-ups, and basically cover all the mundane but important things that a parent will usually do. In residential care, in particular, where there can be as many as thirty staff (obviously depending on the size of the unit and the number of children), it is vital that someone take charge of such things. It is very easy for highly demanding children to claim the lion's share of the attention, while a quieter child can be forgotten. It's also good for a child to have someone to look up to as his/her 'special' worker. Many settings will encourage close relationships between key-worker and key-child. Bonding and attachment are important for any child's development, and that doesn't change because a child is in care.

Bríd was a dour-looking woman in her mid-thirties. She had tightly permed red hair that stood out from her head in what could only be described as an Afro. I was reminded of Luke Kelly *circa* 1972, but Bríd had none of the Red-Haired Minstrel's humour or vivid intellect. She shook my hand and sat opposite me without comment.

Karena was tall and dark-haired, dressed in a hoody and baggy jeans. She looked tired, but she smiled and thanked me for coming.

'Well,' I said when we were all seated and Olwyn and Karena had got coffee for themselves, 'tell me about Larry and Francey.'

'They've been with us now for five weeks,' Olwyn

began. 'They'd been in care for a couple of months by the time we got them, mostly in a series of foster homes. I think that Larry had been through three in that space of time, and Francey had been in two –'

'They'd been separated?'

'Oh, yes. They would never have been inflicted on a family together. They would have been far too challenging.'

'Apologies,' I said. 'I just want to be clear. Carry on.'

'The final foster placements collapsed, and there simply wasn't anywhere else for them to go, so they were sent here. No one seems to have a sense of what we are supposed to be doing with them. We're a long-term setting – our other three children have all been in care since infancy, and the arrival of the twins has turned their world upside-down. I mean, I really can't foresee Larry and Francey remaining here over the long term. They need something that we just can't offer.'

'And what's that, Olwyn?'

'I . . . I think they need psychiatric help. I believe that they're just too disturbed to be in mainstream childcare.'

'You see, Shane', Bríd spoke up in a voice that was practically a monotone, and I noticed that her facial expression never changed, 'the twins are virtually feral in their behaviour. I have enquired from social services as to what their background is and tried to discern what events may have conspired to leave them in this condition, but the details are sketchy. Their family was certainly on the books of the Health Executive for many years, and a Family Support Worker has been involved with them for the past two years. But there was no social-work intervention until the very end, and the written reports from the Family Support Worker are sparse, to say the least.'

'What we do know', Karena continued, 'is that the Byrne family is from Oldtown. The house has been in the family for generations – it's at least a hundred and fifty years old – but has fallen into disrepair. Mrs Byrne has psychiatric problems and Mr Byrne is an alcoholic and a known sex offender. Neighbours state that the Byrne family, while they used to be quite well off, have been . . . how should I put it . . . troubled, for a long time. It is likely that Mr Byrne suffered fairly brutal physical abuse at the very least during his childhood. The Family Support Worker wrote that he could be extremely domineering when he wanted to be. Mrs Byrne seems to be the brains of the operation.'

'The Support Worker's great fear, as it happens', Bríd said, 'was not sexual abuse or even physical abuse, but neglect. The children were failing to thrive. Both are very small for their age and their language development is retarded. Despite fairly intensive speech and language therapy, they *still* speak in a most peculiar fashion, using strange words that seem to me to be outdated, almost medieval. They call a saucepan a "burner", for example, and a screwdriver is a "turn-screw". Their parents don't speak that way, and we don't know why the twins do. That, of course, is when they will speak at all. They regularly revert to non-verbal communication – grunts, snarls, roars and screeches. They will spend all their time out in the grounds if they're allowed, and seem to detest being indoors. I have seen them stalk and kill a pigeon with their bare hands, and, if they manage to get up into one of the trees, they are a nightmare to bring down again.'

I considered this information. There have been around four hundred confirmed cases of feral children throughout recorded history. These are children who have been raised away from human society, either because of enforced isolation by parents or carers, or through losing their family and being raised by animals. There have been a few Irish cases. One was in the seventeenth century, when a boy was raised by sheep in the Wicklow mountains. And there were two in the twentieth century – in both instances the children were placed in chicken coops by abusive parents and raised by the birds. I had researched many of these cases, but had never actually met a feral child. I was fascinated and horrified at the details the workers were giving me. Could this be genuine? Perhaps, as Olwyn had said, the Byrne children were suffering from some psychiatric disorder. I tried not to get carried away. I didn't want my own academic curiosity to lose the run of itself. Even if these two children were truly feral, they were still children, and the most important thing was meeting their needs and helping them.

'You said that there had been no social-work involvement until the children were actually taken into care. How did that happen?'

'A man had come to the house to sell insurance,' Karena said. 'When he knocked on the front door and received no answer, he went to the rear of the building. As he came around the corner, he saw Mr Byrne leading the twins, both naked and covered in cuts and bruises, across the yard to an outhouse. He threw them in and locked the door. The witness reported that he was screaming at them, although he couldn't make out any of the words. Mr Byrne then went back to the house. The insurance salesman returned to his car and called the police.

'They drove out immediately, and found the children in the shed. From the state of the place, it looked as if they had spent a lot of time there. The place stank of shit and piss, the floor was covered in rags and newspaper which the children used as bedding at night, and there were the odd scraps of food their parents would throw in for them to eat. The twins have disclosed that they were often locked up with no food at all for days at a time. They have also hinted at sexual abuse and openly talked about severe beatings. Medical examinations were carried out when they were first taken into care, and they showed that there were many fractures and breaks that had healed, yet there are no records of them ever being hospitalized for anything, or of ever having seen a doctor.'

'They were born in the City Maternity Hospital ten years ago, Shane,' Bríd said. 'I've checked the records. But that is the last time they were seen outside that house. The neighbours did not even know they existed. Why were there no checks from the public health nurse? Why did no one pick up on the fact that they never attended school? We don't know. What we have told you is *all* we know. These are two children who seem to have popped into existence from nowhere.'

'So what we have,' I said, 'are two deeply traumatized children, displaying hugely erratic and challenging behaviour. We only have very sketchy background information, though, and we're faced with a fairly sizeable communication barrier, in that they either won't speak, or speak a language of their own which we can just about understand.'

'That's pretty much it,' Olwyn said.

'What do you want from me?' I asked, a sense of panic, I realized, coming through in my voice.

'A miracle,' Karena smiled, suddenly looking exhausted.

I shook my head. There wasn't really anything to say to that.

'We've been unsuccessful in forming relationships with either of them,' Bríd said. 'The girls have tried very hard, but this is new to all of us, even those of us with experience to fall back on. Benjamin tells me that you have something of an interest in cases like this.'

'I've written a couple of research papers on feral children. As a sociologist, the idea of an individual who is completely unsocialized – who has not been conditioned by human society – is hugely attractive. It's kind of like looking at a person as a blank slate, before language, etiquette and all the rest of the baggage we have has taken hold. I'm fascinated by the phenomenon. I've never actually met a child who *really is* feral, though. I once interviewed a woman who worked with one of the Irish cases, but that's as close as I've got. I think that Ben may have slightly overstated the facts!'

'So you can't help us?' Olwyn said, her voice cracking with emotion.

'Hold on now, I didn't say that,' I said, reaching out and placing a hand on her shoulder. 'What I said was that, while I certainly have an interest and, perhaps, some skills in this field, it's quite new to me too. Now, there are some things we *can* do; some things maybe you haven't thought to try yet. What you need to remember is that flexibility is the key in these situations. If one approach isn't working, there's no shame in trying something else. And besides, even though the children are twins, don't forget that they are still individuals, each with a different psychological make-up. What Larry may respond to, Francey may not.'

'They certainly behave as if they're two parts of the same person,' Karena said. 'It's hard to see them as individuals.'

'It's like they have a pack mentality or something,' Olwyn said, nodding.

'It may appear that way, but it really isn't the case at all. What we need to try and do is unlock that individuality. I don't want to separate them. The bond between twins is remarkably strong, but what we could try to do is have specific times when they *are* separated – perhaps when they have some special time with their key-workers, one-on-one.'

'We never leave a worker alone with them at the moment,' Bríd said. 'They're too difficult to manage. It's always two workers minimum.'

'Maybe I could help there,' I said. 'We can look at scheduling some sessions later.'

'Well, thank you very much, Shane,' Bríd said, almost smiling. 'I'm sure that you'll be a great help.'

She stood. I stood too, and everyone smiled and shook hands with me again.

Bríd led the way back down the stairs, telling me various titbits of information about the religious artefacts that adorned the walls as we descended. It seemed that theological history was something of an interest of hers, and she must have been in heaven in the old hospital with its dark, echoing hallways and countless dusty pictures, statues and ornaments.

'This piece is really fascinating,' she was saying, stopping me by a painting in a guilded frame of Daniel in the Lion's Den. 'It dates back to 1764, I think, and –'

The remainder of her lecture was drowned out by a noise that sounded like a wild-cat roaring, and something sprang from the shadow of the stairwell behind us and landed on Karena's shoulders. The childcare worker screamed in fright and pain and fell to the carpeted floor. Another growl rang out and a second creature dropped from above, this one bouncing off Olwyn and knocking her to the ground. I peered through the murk of the corridor, trying to work out what was happening. The thing on the ground rolled like a monkey and was upright in one fluid motion. I suddenly realized that these must be the Byrnes. What I was looking at were two children. I knew they were ten years of age, but they looked to be much smaller, with masses of light brown hair. Both were naked, and I could see that they still bore the marks of malnutrition and were covered in scars and healing scratches. The child who had felled Olwyn looked at me and hissed like a cat, lashing out at me with clawed hands. I stepped back instinctively.

'Children,' Bríd exclaimed, rushing over to help Olwyn, 'stop this nonsense this instant!'

The child nearest me seemed to be female – her hair was long and unkempt, and it hung right down over her face. She stalked towards me like a predator, long, fluid movements on all fours, rolling from side to side in an almost serpentine pattern. It was very unnerving, and I found myself backing up until I hit the wall. Karena, meanwhile, had pulled herself erect, and she crept behind and scooped up the child into her arms.

'Francey, I want you to go back to bed, please.'

Francey seemed to have other ideas, and with a snarl she sank her teeth into Karena's arm. The worker gasped in pain and momentarily let go her grip, but it was enough time for the child to make the leap to her brother, who was struggling with Bríd and Olwyn. I shook off the sense of panic that had gripped me and ran over, reaching out to restrain the little girl. She must have had good peripheral vision, because, quick as lightning, she swerved to avoid me and, with a howl, leapt over the banisters, vanishing into the darkness to the floor ten feet below us. Larry fought even more ferociously when he saw his sister escape, and in a second had raked Olwyn all down her face and bitten Bríd on the ear. Then he too was gone.

'The Byrnes, I presume,' I said, not sure how I was feeling after the bizarre encounter. I was still reeling from the surreality of it all.

'That's them,' Karena said, examining the marks on poor Olwyn's face.

'Come on, let's see if we can round them up,' Bríd said, and we followed her down the stairs.

We found them in the kitchen. Francey was squatting

under the big, wooden table. Larry was perched on top of it. Milk, cereal and sugar were poured all over the floor in a congealing mess, and both children had fistfuls of bread they were munching on. When Larry saw us enter the room, he gibbered like an ape, jumped up and down a couple of times and then rolled off the table, landing skilfully on his feet and scuttling in beside his sister.

'Larry and Francey,' Bríd said sternly, 'I want you to come out of there and go back to your beds. We will talk about this tomorrow. There will *have* to be sanctions.'

Sanctions is just a nice word for 'punishment'. The twins would have heard it used throughout the few months they'd been in care. I doubted it would cause them to behave any differently. I was right.

Screams and whoops were the only response these remarks received.

I suddenly noticed that the three were standing back, slightly behind me. It seemed they wanted to see what I could do.

'Why don't you try talking to them?' Bríd whispered. 'They might respond better to a stranger.'

Everything I knew about childcare told me this was not true, but I took a deep breath and moved over closer to the table. I hunkered down so that I could see them. They were identical twins, very much alike, the only real differences the varying patterns of the scarring all over their bodies from years of savage beatings, the different sexual organs and the fact that Francey's hair had been kept long, while Larry's had been closely cropped. I scooted over nearer to them so that I was just at the edge

66

of the table, reached into my pocket and took out two sugar-free lollipops. If in doubt, resort to bribery.

'Hey, kids, you don't know me. My name's Shane. Listen, I'm going to be coming here for a while, to hang out with you. I'd like to be friends . . .' I held out the lollipops.

'Isn't this rewarding bad behaviour?' muttered Bríd, loudly enough that the children could hear it.

'No, Bríd, this is me not being judgemental about the behaviour of two obviously distressed children,' I said through gritted teeth. 'Now let me work!'

The twins were eyeing me nervously, lumps of half-chewed bread sticking out of their mouths. I took the plastic wrapping off the lollipops and held them out again. With a loud gulp, Francey swallowed her bread and leaned her head forward, sniffing the air. The posture of the two children was unusual. They were right down on their haunches. Their heads were bent low, so that their shoulders were rounded. Their demeanour suggested that they were far more comfortable on all fours than they were when upright. I heard a trickling, fluid sound, and realized that Francey had just urinated where she was sitting. Her facial expression had not changed. She hadn't voided her bladder from fear – she had done it because she wanted to. The acrid aroma of the urine wafted up to me, but I gave no sign of noticing it. I kept my eyes on the children. Bríd, on the other hand, groaned and sighed loudly, and stomped over to a cupboard, producing a mop. I'm going to have some serious problems with that one, I thought.

'Lookit what him's got there.'

It was said in a whisper, but I caught it.

'Them's sucky sweets, them are.'

Larry had spat out his mouthful of bread and was eyeing the lollipops greedily.

'Him's a quare one,' Francey said quietly. 'Lookit him's longish locks! Him's liken a girl, so he is.'

The speech patterns were indeed peculiar. There were aspects of the kind of dialect children from the traveller community use, but there was a very definite old-fashioned inflection. Their accent was not that of Oldtown; it was almost rural. I was anxious to hear more, and edged forward a little, ducking my head so that I was just under the table too. It was cramped and uncomfortable, and I felt my boots sloshing through Francey's fresh urine, but I was now close enough for them to reach the sweets without having to move out of their bolt-hole.

'You're talking about my long hair,' I said, keeping my tone calm and conversational. 'You haven't seen long hair on a man before?'

They ignored the fact that I was talking, still eyeing me but only addressing each other.

'Him's hair's liken a girly all right,' Larry said. 'But lookit, there's a fuzz outen his face. Girls don't got no fuzz onna their faces, Francey.'

Francey reached out a hand toward the lollipops. I didn't move. She thought better of it for a second, pulling her arm back in, but then seemed to change her mind and edged forward. In a sudden burst of motion she was right up against me, her nose almost at my own. It took all my willpower not to back away from her. She smelt of urine, sour milk and faeces, and her nose and upper lip were caked in mucus. She looked me straight in the eye, then closely examined my beard, reaching out and touching it delicately.

'It's all a-prickly, Lar. Liken a hedgehog!'

Her hand moved to my hair and she 'ooed' and 'aahed' at that.

'It sure is liken a girly. It's all soft and it smells like flowers or perfume bottles and such.'

I stayed perfectly still, letting her explore me in her own way. It was purely primal, like being sniffed by a dog. Babies will do something similar, using touch and smell to get to know a new person.

She pulled back from me slightly and looked me in the eye again.

'You have pretty hair, Francey,' I said. 'I'm sure if you asked Karena, she'd be happy to style it for you. Plaits or something?'

In a movement so fast I didn't see it, she whipped the lollipops from out of my hand and punched me in the face. The strength of the blow was truly remarkable for a child of her size. The pain exploded across the bridge of my nose ('twice in as many days,' I thought ruefully) and I sat down hard, banging my head on the rim of the table as I did so. I felt piss and milk soaking into the back of my jeans and groaned inwardly. Bríd began to say something but I raised an arm to stop her. A thin rivulet of blood dribbled from my left nostril and over my moustache, but I wiped it off with the back of my hand. It seemed that I had crossed a line with Francey – had spoken out of turn. However, I could not permit the act of aggression to pass uncommented upon. I needed to start as I intended to continue.

'Francey, I know you're upset right now – I can see that very clearly. Because you don't know me, and because you're frightened, I'm going to let the fact that you hit me pass, just this once. But you need to know, when you're with me, I have just two rules. You don't hurt anyone, not yourself and not me, and you try your best. I won't hurt you, and I expect you to treat me the same way. Is that clear?'

The sounds of furious sucking came from the other end of the table. The twins' eyes were wide now – they were listening to me all right.

'I'd like you to answer me please, Francey. When I speak, I like it when people speak back to me. It's rude to ignore a person when they talk to you.'

'You can just take your rules and your smelly hair and fuck right off wit yourself,' Francey said around the sweet. 'That's allen I has to say to ya, okay?'

I grinned. 'It's better than nothing.' I stood up, massaging the small of my back. 'Let's clean up here, ladies. I trust that the cupboards and drawers can all be locked and secured?'

The three women nodded, and mutely began to clean away the mess the twins had created and to lock all the food-stores and cutlery drawers. Within ten minutes, other than the silent presence under the table, you would never have known that the Byrnes had been there. I poured a basin of soapy water down the sink, and then hunkered down by the table again.

'Kids, we're going into the living room to watch some

TV. You have two choices. You can stay here, or you can come in, have a cup of tea with us and then go to bed. To be honest, I don't mind which you do. I'm sure you're both really nice kids, but you haven't been very good company this evening. My nose is sore and I have a bit of a headache, and before we sit down to watch any television, Olwyn is going to have to put some antiseptic ointment on her face. You are responsible for those things. I'm not mad at you, and I don't think Olwyn is either [Olwyn muttered that she wasn't] and there'll be no more said about it, but when you make a decision to hurt someone, you need to realize what it is that you're doing. I'd like you to think about that, while you make up your minds what you'd like to do now.'

I motioned to the three staff members and we left the room.

'Do you think it was wise to let them know they hurt us?' Olwyn asked, as Karena led the way to the TV room.

'Why not?' I said. 'We aren't robots. We're people. People get hurt when you punch or scratch them. They need to understand that. By the look of them, they've had plenty of violence directed at them. They were probably expected to take it and pass no remark. The real world isn't like that. Cut me, and I bleed. I have no problem with the Byrnes knowing it.'

We all took chairs (I chose a wooden one, since my jeans were by now reeking of urine) and Bríd went to get the first-aid kit. Karena turned on the television with the volume down low, and we waited.

Fifteen minutes later, two dejected-looking figures

appeared in the doorway. Olwyn silently went past them to fetch their pyjamas.

'Now, kids,' Karena said gently, 'would ye like some supper or have you had enough to eat?'

'We'd liken some tay, so we would,' Francey said, eyeing me with real venom.

'I'll put the kettle on,' Bríd said.

They drank their tea quietly and went to bed without much protest. I watched them all the while, still unsure of what I was really seeing. They were an enigma. I just hoped that I would be able to unlock the secret that was hidden within these untamed, violent children.

5

One week later

Through the kitchen window, I watched Bobby and Micky Walsh talking to something that wasn't there. It was a disquieting experience. The kitchen, as always, was in semi-darkness. With Biddy's permission, I had been through the house to see if I could do anything about the pervasive gloom that seemed to cocoon it. It was a beautiful summer's day outside, but inside was dark and actually a little chilly. I had washed all the windows thoroughly, made tie-backs for the curtains and aired the place, but the eternal twilight remained and there was a peculiar smell I just couldn't get rid of. I had finally put it down to a design flaw in the building. The sun always seemed to be shining just at the wrong angle.

I watched the two boys closely. This was the first time that Biddy had allowed me to see them when they were with 'him', and permission had been granted only when I promised not to intrude upon whatever was happening.

The boys' eyes were fixed at a particular point in the air. The brothers were different heights; Micky, as I've already mentioned, was significantly smaller than Bobby. He had to angle his head much more than his sibling, and I thought he would surely get bored with it and look away, but he didn't. They both continued to focus on a patch of air, around six feet above ground level. I looked to see if there was some point of reference for them, a mark on the wall at that point or a branch from the ditch adjacent to them, but, if there was, I couldn't see it. It was simply a patch of empty air.

I couldn't hear what was being said. The windows were double-glazed and no sound came through, but I could see from the boys' body-language that they were having an animated conversation – although not with each other. Bobby would speak, and there would be a pause. Both boys, seated cross-legged on the ground, would talk together, just as they would if they were speaking to me or their mother, but then one would shout the other down, finish saying his piece, wait again, all the time looking at something I couldn't see. It really did look for all the world as if they were talking to, listening to, responding to an invisible person.

The play-work had so far produced nothing. I'd tried a range of different methodologies – sand and water, clay, role-play, storytelling – but I was beginning to see that the boys were not going through a grieving process at all, because, as far as they were concerned, *their father was not dead!* Their behaviour with me was always pleasant and respectful. To be honest, I had fun with them. They were easy to work with and I looked forward to coming over and spending time with them. When the subject of their father came up, which it did at almost every session, they behaved as if their relationship with him was perfectly normal. I asked them on my third visit how they knew when to go out to the garden to see him.

'I hears him calling us,' Micky said. 'He shouts "*Micheál! Micheál!*" and I goes out and there he is, down by the ditch.'

'Do you hear it like that too, Bob?'

'No, he calls to Micky.'

'Do you not hear him calling then?'

'No, but I sees him when we goes out there. I loves my daddy.'

'Boys . . . do you know your daddy is dead?'

This may seem a terribly blunt statement, but a primary rule in childcare is that you are always truthful with the children you work with. I wanted them to see that, from my point of view at least, their father was not there. The boys stopped making the castle they had been building in the sand-tray I had brought over and looked at me solemnly.

'No,' Bobby said with firm resolution. 'You see, Shane, that was a mistake. Daddy told us he wasn't ready to be dead. They made a mistake.'

'Weren't you ever at his grave?'

'No.' Micky shook his head vigorously. 'There idn't any grave, cause he's ain't dead.'

And that had been the end of the conversation on that matter. As far as both boys were concerned, their father was very much alive and well.

I watched the drama unfolding outside with rapt fascination. I had absolutely no idea how the hallucination worked. I did, however, know one thing for certain: *they were seeing something*. Of that I was in no doubt.

My mobile phone rang.

'Yeah.'

'Hi, Shane. Ben here. Could you swing by the Henrys as soon as possible? Mina has done a bunk again.'

'No problem. I'm just about done here anyway.'

Dirk Henry sat in his study behind a huge oak desk, a glass of whiskey in his hand and a cigar smouldering between his teeth. He had come home from work to meet me, so he was dressed in an immaculately tailored grey suit. He was not in a good mood.

I don't know what he did for a living. He had snorted at me that he was involved in finance. I thought that that was a pretty broad field of endeavour, but kept the opinion to myself.

'We did as you suggested, Shane, and operated the alarm system.'

'And?'

'It worked. She has not escaped from the house.'

I waited, saying nothing. Dirk was obviously used to chairing meetings, and he had a flair for the dramatic. I knew that a punch line was coming, and I gave him the opportunity to deliver it in his own time.

'She ran away from the workshop this morning.'

It made sense. If one avenue of escape was cut off, Mina was always going to look for another one.

'You didn't think to inform the workshop that she maybe needed to be watched?'

Dirk's eyes narrowed. 'I would have thought that was your job,' he said very quietly.

I shrugged. Dirk was probably used to having employees tremble when he squinted like that and lowered his voice. But I wasn't his employee, and men in suits have rarely frightened me. I stood up.

'Where are you going?'

'To look for your daughter.'

'Where the hell are you planning to look?'

'Well, I'm going to begin by going over to the workshop to see if anyone there had any ideas, seeing as there seems to be something of a shortage of them around here.'

'What's that supposed to mean?'

'It means that I want to begin looking for Mina, and that I'm not prepared to sit around here any longer while you make yourself feel better by showing me how tough you are.'

I left him chewing on that, and went out to the car, feeling quite pleased with myself. Which probably made me just as childish as him.

Community workshops for people with special needs all look alike, built to the same basic design. I think they're supposed to appear welcoming, but to me they all seem like factories, and there is nothing welcoming about that. Workshops are supposed to be about something called *industrial therapy*. That's supposed to mean that people can receive healing or personal development through work. I spent some time in a workshop once, on the floor, just like one of the 'trainees', as they call the individuals with disabilities who work there. I had been offered a job as a supervisor, but first wanted to see what it was like from the trainee's perspective. I asked if I could do a week putting together industrial cables, which was what the particular room I was supposed to be supervising made. The manager looked at me as if I had just sprouted a second head, but agreed. I lasted for one day, by the end of which I thought I was about to go insane. I never took up the job. I could not stand over asking anybody, special needs or not, to do something I was not prepared to do myself. Since then, I have always thought that *industrial therapy* just means cheap labour.

'Mina came in this morning as normal,' Brendan, the manager of the workshop, told me.

He was a beefy man with a large paunch and the huge shoulders of a body-builder. We sat in his tiny, stuffy office, overlooking the floor of the workshop.

'How'd she run off?'

He sighed and rubbed the back of his neck with a grubby-looking handkerchief. He was sweating profusely.

'Security has never been much of an issue here, Shane. Our people just don't run away. Most of them are actually afraid to go outside on their own. In general they lead fairly sheltered lives, so the door is never locked. No one ever told me that Mina was a flight risk. If I'd known . . .'

'I'm not here to point the finger of blame, Brendan. That's kind of a pointless exercise at this stage. The horse has bolted.'

'Yeah, well I feel bad about it.'

'You'll be more careful next time. Could be something you and your people need to develop some policies on, eh?'

'Maybe.'

'Would you say Mina's happy here?'

Brendan looked at me blankly. 'I don't follow.'

'Do you think she enjoys her time here – doing the work, being with the people?'

'Well, I think so. She's never complained.'

'Do you get many complaints from the trainees, Brendan?'

'Well . . . um . . . no, I s'pose not.'

'Who does Mina hang out with? Does she have any particular friends?'

'Have you ever worked with special needs, Shane?'

'Yes.'

'Then you'll know that they don't really have friends. Not in any real sense. They'll latch on to members of staff, have favourites that way, but they tend not to develop close relationships with one other.'

'That has not been my experience.'

'Oh, well, it's what I've seen.'

'Thank you for your time. Can I go down to the floor and chat with a few of the trainees? They might know something that could help.'

'Yeah, no bother. You'll not learn much, though.'

I smiled without humour and went down the flight of metal stairs to where the trainees worked. The workshop was divided up into different sections. There was an area that did screen-printing, a facility that packaged plastic bin-liners, one that made synthetic clothes lines and another that produced craft-work – various knick-knacks and oddments. Mina worked in this last section, so I made my way across the large room to where I had been told her work-station was. The atmosphere of the place was pleasant enough. It was light and airy and there was a buzz of conversation along with the clang of

79

machinery. The craft department was cordoned off from its neighbouring section by a wooden partition. I introduced myself to the supervisor, who told me her name was Ellen. She had a Northern accent and was a pretty, dark-haired woman in her early thirties.

'Do you mind if I chat to the guys here, and see if anyone has any idea where Mina's run off to?'

'Aye, that's fine. We're dead worried about her. I only noticed she was gone when we came back from tea-break. It's not at all like her. She's such a conscientious wee lass.'

'Any thoughts yourself as to where she might have gone?'

'Jesus, no, none at all. She's a quiet girl really. She never says a whole lot.'

'She hasn't mentioned anything out of the ordinary, something that made you stop and think?'

'No. Sorry. Sure, have a chat with the lads; they might be able to help.'

'Could you introduce me?'

'Of course.'

Ellen walked to the centre of the work area and held up a hand. The people working at their desks all put down the pieces they were busy with and looked up.

'This is Shane. He's here to ask ye about Mina, who, as you all know, has gone away without telling anyone where she was heading. Shane would like to ask each of you if you have any thoughts on where she might have gone to, seeing as how you're all her friends. So please do tell him anything you think will help.'

The trainees looked warily at one another and returned to their work.

There were six people in this section. Some said that they knew Mina well, while others said they had barely spoken to her. After forty-five minutes, I was ready to give up in frustration. The last member of the team was a man in his forties, Hughie, who seemed to have a slightly more severe learning disability than his colleagues. He wore thick eye-glasses with black plastic frames, and he looked directly over my shoulder as I spoke to him, never at my face. He rocked quite violently during our conversation. I got the impression that he was rarely at ease, and that I was adding greatly to his discomfort. I decided to keep the conversation as brief as possible.

'Hughie, do you and Mina ever chat at all?'

'What? Me and Mina? Oh, yeah . . . yeah . . . we're good friends, me and Mina. Good friends we are.'

'Has she ever told you about places she likes to go?'

'Yeah . . . yeah . . . Mina likes to go . . . likes to go to the workshop to be with her friends. To be with Hughie.'

'What about other places?'

'Likes to go to the Abled-Disabled Club. I go there – Hughie goes there too. We dance to the music and we play games.'

'That's nice, Hughie. That sounds like a lot of fun.'

'Yeah!' he laughed out loud and his rocking became even more erratic. 'Hughie has fun at the Abled-Disabled Club! Fun!'

'Is there anywhere else she likes to go, Hughie?'

'My daddy brings me for a pint on a Sunday after Mass!

Hughie likes to go for a pint. A pint of Guinness and a ball of malt.'

'I wouldn't say no to a pint myself right about now, Hughie, I'll tell you that much.'

'And Mina goes for a pint in The Sailing Cot.'

The Sailing Cot? The name suggested a waterfront setting, and Garibaldi Street, where Mina and her parents lived, was nowhere near the river.

'Are you sure about that, Hughie? She likes to go to a pub called The Sailing Cot?'

'Oh yeah. Pints in The Sailing Cot. Mina says that.'

I said my good-byes and rang Dirk from the car.

'Have you ever brought Mina to a pub called The Sailing Cot?'

'No. I've never heard of such a place.'

'Have you ever heard her mention it?'

'No.'

'Okay. I'll get back to you.'

I had never heard of a pub with that name either, but the landlord of my local told me that there was a Sailing Cot down on the waterfront, by the docks. When I asked him what kind of a place it was, he looked uncomfortable and said that it wouldn't be *his* choice of hostelry, and that he'd be surprised if I liked it. I told him I'd give him a thorough report, and, as early evening began to fall on the city, I headed for the docklands.

I found the pub eventually. It was a small place, halfway up an alley. A swinging sign, covered in grime and soot, depicting a sail-boat being tossed on a stormy sea, hung from two rusty chains at the mouth of the alley. The smell of the tidal river hung heavily in the air, and cranes and fork-lifts moved noisily on the busy docks. On the waterfront, business kept going twenty-four hours a day. I could hear the shouts of the workers, many different accents and languages mingling. This was not a place the Henrys would have ever come to. In fact, I thought as I stood outside the door of the pub, with its cracked paint and ageing posters advertising Sweet Afton cigarettes, that this was not a place I would ever come to. But there I was. So I pushed open the door, paused as the stench of stale beer, cigarette smoke and body odour washed over me, and went in.

Inside it was so dark I had to pause again as my eyes adjusted. There was a small bar facing me, and the rest of the room was divided into cubicles and snugs. An elderly man in a shirt that had probably started out life white, but was now grey, stood leaning on the bar. A cigarette smouldered in the corner of his mouth, a long strand of greasy yellow hair was brushed over his bald pate and he badly needed a shave. I could hear murmurs and muted conversation from the snugs, but the shadows were so deep I couldn't make out anyone.

'Can I help you, sir?' the barman asked, smiling and displaying very few teeth.

'I'll have a sparkling water, please. Ice and lemon.'

His smile broadened. 'A water. For the chap.'

'Please.'

'We don't have ice. Don't get much call for it.'

'Warm will be fine.'

He produced a dusty bottle from beneath the bar without ever taking his eyes off me, and then reached behind him and took a surprisingly clean glass from the shelf.

'Thanks,' I said, and poured for myself. 'I'm looking for someone I've been told comes in here. A young woman.'

'Sir, the girls work outside. We don't allow them in. It's bad for business.'

'No, no. This is a friend of mine. A girl with Down's Syndrome.'

'Wha'?'

'Ummm . . . she's got a disability . . . she looks different . . . y'know.'

'You mean the mongoloid girl.'

'Yes! Have you seen her?'

'Did she come in this evenin' now? I think she did. Have you looked over in the snug over there? That's where she usually goes.'

'Thank you. Does she come in on her own?'

'Oh no,' the barman laughed. 'Never alone. She has a bit of an eye for the fellas, does that one. I wouldn't like a girl like that meself now . . . don't get me wrong, I've nothin' agin it, but,' he leaned towards me and whispered, 'what would the children be like? Would they be handicapped or normal?'

I put the glass on the bar and turned away from him. The bar seemed to be uncomfortably hot, the air too thin.

'You think she might be over there?'

'The middle snug. There isn't goin' to be trouble, is there?'

'I hope not.'

The distance to the snug was only about six feet, but

it seemed to take me for ever to cross it. I stood at the door of the cubicle and looked in, not knowing what to expect.

The snug was lit by one bare light bulb that was not on a wire; the socket was fitted into the low ceiling. There was a small table in the centre, upon which was a pint-glass with the dregs of Guinness in it, and a glass that contained a short of some kind. There were soft seats on either side of the table, the upholstery worn and the stuffing showing through in places. On one of these seats sat Mina, draped around a man in his late fifties. He was a skinny, angular individual, his chin and cheeks covered in a salt-and-pepper stubble. He wore a dirty blue suit that was far too big for him, under which he had a purple cardigan and a yellow shirt. His hair hung in strands around his shoulders, black streaked with grey. He looked up at me and smiled. The smile made him look cadaverous and predatory at the same time. Mina had not looked at me, although I was sure she knew I was there.

'I've come for my friend,' I said to the man, fighting to keep the anger from my voice.

'We're all friends, here, Mister,' the thin man said, kissing Mina on the cheek and wrapping his arm around her, leaving his hand resting on her breast.

'I want you to take your hands off her and walk out of here right now,' I said through clenched teeth.

'And why exactly would that be?'

'She is a child. Her parents want her home. I don't believe that she wants to be here with you – and I'm telling you to leave.'

'She's no child. Look at her. This is no baby here, Mister.'

I felt bile rising and clenched my fists.

'She is only seventeen years old.'

'Old enough, as I understand the law, to make up her own mind.'

'Mina, come on, we're leaving.'

I reached out my hand to her, and for the first time she looked at me. Her brown eyes were huge and wet, but I couldn't read what was in them. The thin man, seeing what was happening, leant around her and kissed her full on the mouth, pushing his tongue between her lips. I rushed at them, grabbing him by the scruff of the neck and heaving him away from her. He threw a punch at me, but I had him off balance and the blow went wide, bouncing off the wall. I pulled Mina to her feet and pushed her behind me. She came placidly. The thin man lay on the seat, fury burning in his eyes at having the prey snatched from his grasp.

'I'll see you soon, Mina,' he said, smiling again. He looked at me, and the smile left his face. 'And I'll be seeing you too. Watch your back, Mister.'

I shook my head in disgust and led Mina from the snug. Two men were now at the bar – they didn't look like bouncers, but I had the impression that that was their purpose. The bartender had a decidedly unhappy look about him. There was no muttered conversation. All eyes followed us as we walked to the door.

'Bye, Mina,' the thin man called as we left.

I didn't stop, but walked as fast as I could to where I had parked. Mina was silent beside me, but her pace was quick and she didn't try to shrug off my arm. I fumbled with my keys (my hands were still shaking) and unlocked the passenger-side door. She got in and sat there, looking ahead, as if in a daze. I walked quickly to my own side of the car and was just about to open the door when I stopped dead.

Directly across the street, about one hundred yards from the alley where The Sailing Cot plied its trade, was a corner where two roads conjoined. On this corner stood a group of four girls. They were dressed in short skirts and strappy tops, all revealing a bare midriff, and each of them wore knee-high boots with high heels. The corner was not a bus-stop, and I didn't think that they were waiting for a taxi either. Given the area I was in, the time of evening and the dress and demeanour of the girls, it was obvious what their purpose was. What stopped me in my tracks was that I thought I recognized one of the girls. The group was only a few yards away, and there was still enough light to see them clearly, but it had been years since I had seen this girl. I looked again. Yes, it was her!

Her name was Sylvie. I had worked with her in a residential children's home while I was still a student. As a student, I was not permitted to act as a key-worker, but I had developed a very close bond with her, nonetheless. She had called me her 'minder' – her protector. At that time she had just been taken into care, the victim of a psychiatrically disturbed mother, abandoned by her father, and the experience had been a traumatic one for her. I used to read to her before she went to bed, an activity we both looked forward to. She had loved the story of Cinderella – especially the notion of having a fairy godmother, someone watching over you and looking after you all the time. She asked me one evening, snuggled up on my knee as I read her the story, if I believed there really was such a thing as a fairy godmother. I told her that, yes, I liked to think that there was. The world had never been kind to Sylvie, and she needed all the comfort she could get. Judging by what I was seeing, her fairy godmother had been sorely negligent in her duties.

I did some quick sums in my head. She had been four when I had worked with her. That meant that now she couldn't be much more than thirteen. As I watched, a couple of men walked up and stopped to talk to the girls. I was torn: I could not handle Mina and this waif at the same time. I hadn't seen Sylvie in almost ten years – she may not even have remembered me. She would never have come with me right off. I would have had to talk to her for an hour or more, and even then it might have been a waste of time. I wasn't even a hundred per cent certain she *was* on the game, although it was starting to look more and more like a dead cert. Cursing myself for what I had to do, I got in and drove away without looking back. Sylvie would have to wait.

Mina would neither look at me nor speak to me on the drive home. I tried talking to her for a while, then gave up and focused on my own thoughts. I pushed Sylvie to the back of my mind, and considered what had just happened with Mina. My head was awhirl with the possibilities, none of which was good. Had Mina been running away to meet that man? Was she having a relationship with him? Had he in some manner inveigled his way into the Abled-Disabled Club or the workshop and coerced her into a sexual relationship? Had she just run into him by accident this afternoon, and they had got together? She was obviously a regular in The Sailing Cot. How had she even found the place? What had brought her there initially? She was, according to the barman, known as having 'an eye for the fellas'. Was she purposely going out to meet men? I had no answers to any of these questions, and Mina was not making any effort to enlighten me. I pulled up outside her house, and she opened the door and got out without a word. I followed her up the drive and waited while her mother answered the door.

Mina shot past her and straight up the stairs. Her mother stood at the door, her mouth open, gazing after her daughter and then looking back at me.

'My God . . . you . . . you found her!'

'Can we go inside and sit down, Molly? I need to talk to you both, and what I have to say isn't pretty.'

She showed me into the living room, where Dirk was already standing, looking pale and worried.

'Thank you for bringing my daughter home, Shane. About this afternoon . . .'

'Let's not go over that, Dirk. I was as much an ass as you were. Just listen to me now. There's some things we need to go over.'

I told them how I had found Mina, what had happened in the grotty pub by the river, and described the thin man. They sat through it all, never saying a word. When I was finished, Dirk, whose Adam's apple had been bobbing like a cork in a basin of water, swallowed and took a deep breath.

'Well, I'm devastated. I don't know what to say.'

'I'm sorry to have to bring you such bad news.'

'Well, she's home now.'

'Yes. I don't think that there would be any point in trying to talk to her just at the moment. Let her have her space. I'll come by tomorrow. Perhaps she'll talk to you in the meantime, but I doubt it. Let's just hope she opens up soon. There are a lot of questions that need answering.'

'Oh, I'm sure she's got whatever it is out of her system, Shane. I doubt that we'll have any more trouble with her now.'

'I don't know. I wish I could agree, but there's something odd happening. I don't know what it is yet. There are just too many coincidences. Nothing adds up.'

'I'd really prefer it if we just leave it, Shane,' Molly said.

I had almost forgotten she was there. I looked over at her, and saw that she was crying. I felt for her, but I was strongly getting the sense that neither of them was surprised by this turn of events. They were desperately embarrassed that I had tracked her down, horrified that I knew the dirty little secret, but not at all surprised that I had found their daughter in a clinch with a filthy man in a seedy pub in a dangerous part of the city.

'With respect, Molly, we *can't* leave it. Mina has been going out and, intentionally or under duress, I don't know which, has been giving herself to men. And not nice, pleasant, gentlemen, but men who want to use her, who want to take advantage of this vulnerable young woman. Now I don't think that we can just pretend that this hasn't happened. We need to talk to her about it, have her medically checked out to see that she hasn't picked up any sexually transmitted infections, maybe get her some counselling. There are courses, specially designed for people with intellectual disabilities, called "body awareness programmes", which can help Mina to have a better understanding of her sexuality. We have a huge range of things to do now. This is just the beginning.'

'Thank you for your help, Shane.' Dirk stood up and extended his hand. 'I think Molly and I had best be getting off to bed. It's been a trying day for all of us.'

At the door I turned and looked him hard in the eye.

'I don't know what's going on here, Dirk. But I do know that Mina is hurting, and that she seems to be trapped in a cycle of behaviour that is going to end up with her being hurt a whole lot more. Don't try and brush it under the carpet. The only way to deal with this is to talk about it.'

He looked at me for a moment, and I thought he was going to answer me. I could see that he was fighting to keep his composure, that he was on the edge of collapsing. But he just cleared his throat, patted me firmly on the shoulder and said: 'Goodnight, Shane.'

I sat in the car and lit up a cigarette. Night had come down, and the street-lights shed a sickly yellow glow over the finely manicured street. I felt tired and old. But there was one final thing I had to do before I could go home. Now that Mina was safe, my thoughts turned to Sylvie. I swung the car around, and went back to the docks.

*

The corner where the four girls had been was empty. I parked up the street a bit and switched off the engine. The docks still thundered on with the sounds of people whose lives revolved around better, brighter things. I switched on the radio, fiddled with the dial and found a jazz programme. Charles Mingus hollered *Hog Call Blues* out of the speakers. Not exactly gentle, but good. I sat and smoked and waited. The glow from the street-lamps was just as yellow here as it had been on Garibaldi Street. People came and went, but the girls appeared to be long gone. I waited another hour and then went home, cursing myself all the way.

When I got back to my apartment, I opened all the windows to let in some air. The sounds of the street filtered up, and somehow that made me seem less alone. I felt soiled and grimy. I dug out Mingus's *Oh Yeah* and put it on loud, then went into the shower and stood under the spray for almost an hour. Wrapped in a towel, I made a long drink and sat on the couch in the dark as the music played and the night dragged on and somewhere out there a little girl who had once thought of me as her minder did tricks for freaks. Sometime after midnight I slept. If I dreamed, I don't remember.

PART TWO

Wayfaring Stranger

I am a wayfaring stranger
Travelling through this world of woe.
And neither toil, nor grief, nor danger
Are in this world to which I go.
I'm going there to see my father
And all my loved ones who've gone on
I'm just going over Jordan;
I'm just going over home.

Poor Wayfaring Stranger, TRADITIONAL FOLK SONG
(FROM THE SINGING OF JOHNNY CASH)

6

Sunlight, in a concentrated beam full of swirling dust-motes, came into the office I shared with Loretta. The window looked out on the overgrown rear garden, the tumbling vines and swaying, sinuous shrubs a mirror of my inner chaos.

It was just before nine in the morning, and I didn't know if Loretta would be in. I had called to Dunleavy House only a couple of times since taking up the job, and so had no idea of my colleagues' routines. A pile of just-opened post sat at my elbow, all of it reports and documentation on my three cases: articles of information which were missing from the files Ben had given me. I sorted them into chronological order and put them in their relevant folders. It took me ten minutes, and then I sat there, wondering what the hell else I could do. Administration has never been my strong suit, but I felt that I should be doing something. I had come in early to write up a report on the previous day's experiences with Mina and the Walshes, which proved to be a short job. I finally accepted that there wasn't really anything else for me to do, and went to get a coffee.

Benjamin was seated in the kitchen when I went in, reading *The Irish Times*, drinking a cup of green tea and eating a muffin.

'There you are,' he said as I went to the coffee machine. 'How has it been going?'

I sat opposite him and ran a hand through my hair, sighing deeply.

'Slower than I'd like, if I'm honest.'

'They're three difficult cases. You have them because you have the necessary skills. You'll get there.'

'Thanks for the vote of confidence.'

'What do you make of the Byrnes?'

'Have you met them?'

'I meet all the children who get referred to us.'

'Then you'll know that they are a complete mess.'

'I knew you'd like them,' he smiled, sipping his tea and popping a piece of muffin into his mouth.

'I'll admit that I'm fascinated.' I paused, my mind suddenly full of questions I wanted to ask Ben. 'Do you think it's accurate to say that they're feral children? I mean, the term "feral" in this context really means *unsocialized*.'

Socialization, as I mentioned earlier, is the process of learning how to behave in a society through *living within* that society. It involves all the things we learn from our parents: language, how to eat using a knife and fork, toilet training; as well as the patterns of behaviour we pick up from the wider community: moral codes, religion and fashion trends, to mention but a few.

'They *have* language of a kind,' I continued. 'I think that it's fairer to say that what they really lack are social skills.'

'What about the fact that they run about on all fours?'

'Not all the time. They walk upright far more often. Part of me has been wondering if they affect the animalistic behaviour to scare people. The snarls, the clawing, that whole pattern seems to me to be more a defence mechanism. Who's going to want to fuck with two wolf-children?'

'I'd go for that if it didn't seem so ingrained,' Benjamin said. 'You can't just decide to play at being a were-wolf or a monkey or whatever it is they're meant to be, and within a couple of months be able to catch wild birds with your bare hands. It's an interesting theory, and I think it may have *become* a defensive behaviour, but my bet is that there's something much deeper at work.'

'Any suggestions as to how to isolate it, so that we can begin to form relationships with them, because, as of a couple of days ago, things have not improved one iota?'

'What have you been trying?'

'Well, based on the knowledge that they've been confined in a shed for long periods of time and seem to get very edgy and claustrophobic when cooped up indoors, I've been working with them outside. They're certainly happier outdoors – the problem is that Rivendell has fairly big grounds, and once they get outside they're off like wildfire, usually ending up perched in a tree. Their two key-workers have been attending the sessions, seeing as how they're the ones who are constants in the children's lives, and they've both worked really hard, but they're getting frustrated. I spent the last session halfway up a goddam conifer, talking to the twins.'

'Only halfway up?'

'The branches wouldn't hold my weight any higher, Ben. Larry and Francey are undersized for their age. They can sit on twigs and not break them.'

'How has the violence been since you got involved?'

'I don't think there's been anything major since that first night.'

'And wouldn't you call that progress?'

'I'd love to, but I think that what's happening is that they're running off all their energy out in the garden, tormenting us.'

'Don't sell yourself short. Keep doing what you're doing. Sounds to me like they may be taking in more than they're letting on.'

'You reckon?'

'I'd be very surprised if there isn't some kind of break-through within the next week or so. You've been staying with it, even when they've made it difficult for you. They punched you in the face, and instead of running away, you came back for more. They climb up a tree, you climb up after them. You have made more of an effort to be their friend than anyone else has, and, in doing so, you've brought along those key-workers, who by extension have shown the desire to work with the twins regardless of how badly they behave. The twins will have noticed, and are probably quite puzzled. They're waiting for the bubble to burst, expecting someone to resort to violence. It'll take time for them to realize that no one in Rivendell will do that to them.'

'Well, I hope that it happens soon, because Olwyn and Karena are starting to lose all faith in me. They seemed to think that I would come on board, wave a magic wand and make everything all right. They've been sorely disappointed.'

'Perhaps you need to give them more credit than that.

They know that there are no certainties. Have you asked them how they've experienced the sessions so far?'

'Olwyn has more often than not been in tears by going-home time. Karena is always very quiet.'

'You should probably be doing some debriefing with them. Treat them like your team. Don't neglect them because you're worried about what they're thinking of you.'

'You're right. I'll have a coffee with them after today's session.'

'Why not do it first? Take some time, let them vent at you. Give *them* a session if you feel they need it. You've been working closely alongside these people now for a week or so. I'd say it's time to talk with them, wouldn't you?'

I nodded and drained the last of my coffee. He was right, as usual. I'd been full of angst about what these childcare workers – my peers, effectively – were making of my painstakingly slow progress, and as a result I had neglected to communicate with them, despite the fact that they were finding the work so difficult. My focus was *supposed* to be on the children, but not to the detriment of their staff.

'I'll do that. Thanks, Ben.'

'No problem. Look, you have my number. Let's meet for a pint some night. D'you still play music?'

'Yeah, when I can find the time.'

'There's a great little session on Crabbe Street, in The Minstrel Boy. Why don't you come along next week, and I'll introduce you. We could do with another musician.

There's no money, but they'll stand us a few pints if they're in a good mood.'

I grinned. 'That would be really great.'

My mobile phone rang, a number I didn't know flashing on the display. I apologized to Benjamin and answered it.

'Yeah?'

'Shane, it's Olwyn.'

I could tell straight away that she had been crying, but then that wasn't unusual for her, so I didn't put much pass on it.

'Hey, Olwyn. I'm due to come out and see you later. Is there anything up?'

She was sobbing.

'I've fucked up, Shane. I've fucked up badly. I don't know what to do.'

'Okay. Where are you now?'

'I'm not on shift until midday. I'm at home.'

'Where do you want to meet me?'

'Not here. I live with my mam.'

'No problem. What about The People's Park? We can walk and you can tell me what's happened. See you in half an hour by the fountain?'

'Thanks. I'll be there.'

She looked subdued and pale. She hadn't bothered with the Gothic make-up, and was dressed in a simple blue T-shirt and jeans. I had brought along two cardboard cups of take-out coffee and some doughtnuts. She took the coffee, thanking me, but shook her head at the pastries.

'So what's up?'

'Oh God, it's hard. I've done something terrible.'

'Hold on now. In childcare, because the stakes are so high, when we go wrong it always seems like it's the worst kind of mistake that anyone could possibly make. And you know what? It rarely is. So start from the beginning, and tell me what's happened since I saw you last.'

She started to sob again and I put my arms around her. We stood there in the middle of the pathway and I didn't say anything. There was no one else in the park except for a couple of dog-walkers, and they gave us a wide berth, embarrassed by the girl's noisy unhappiness. To hell with them, I thought. They'd forget about us as soon as they'd gone past. After five or six minutes, she stepped back from me, wiping her nose and rubbing her eyes like a child. I took her arm and led her to a park-bench. She was fruitlessly searching for a tissue, so I pulled a small plastic packet from my pocket and handed it to her.

I sat back and waited, sipping my coffee. A robin perched on a shrub near us and watched me with intense curiosity. Robins look cute and cuddly, but are in fact fiercely territorial birds, living a life packed with violence and aggression. Just like our society really. Beautiful on the surface, but scratch just a little beneath . . .

'After you visited, two days ago,' Olwyn said at last, 'we took all the kids out for a drive to the beach. It was nice, actually. Larry and Francey behaved very well. The other children still keep them at arm's length, but there were no outbursts.'

'Sounds like fun.'

'Yeah, it was. We stayed a little bit away from the

crowd, just for safety's sake, but a young couple came up the beach, walking. They had a toddler with them. Each of them was holding one of his hands – they had to bend down to do it. He had a little sun-suit on, with a floppy hat to keep the sun off his eyes, and he was gorgeous, a really happy little fella. His parents obviously doted on him. None of our kids paid them a blind bit of notice, except Larry. He sat there, his eyes glued to them. He watched them for ages. He never said anything, but you could tell that something was bothering him.'

'Hard thing for him to see, I suppose. He was never loved like that.'

'Larry was quiet on the way back to Rivendell. Said nothing all through dinner. Then, just before bed, he called me in to his room. I was surprised. I always go in, to say goodnight, but he usually just ignores me. He'd never called me in before. In fact, short of calling me names, he'd never really spoken to me. "Olly," he says, "can I have a picture of you?" I was dumbstruck. I didn't know what to say.'

'What did you do?'

'We'd taken some snaps on a trip out the previous week, and I got him one with the two of us in it. He said thanks, and took it – and then he gave me a hug.'

All Larry's previous physical contact with staff had been hostile. An expression of affection like this was momentous; it was a breakthrough.

'Congratulations! That's brilliant.'

'You haven't heard it all yet,' Olwyn said, tears beginning to run down her cheeks again.

'Okay, take your time.'

'The next morning – the day before yesterday – he came out of his room clutching the photo. He followed me around all morning. Every time I turned, he was there. I was due to go off shift at lunchtime, but he kept me hanging around for at least an hour more, behaving in a way none of us had ever seen before. He was all hugs and cuddles and seemed at times to be almost showing off. He wanted me to look at him running and doing somersaults on the lawn. Francey was not at all happy. She wanted nothing to do with it. When I finally managed to extricate myself, he ran over, threw his arms around me and said: "Bye, Mammy." I nearly had a heart attack.'

'What did you do?'

She choked back a sob.

'I hugged him and went home.'

My heart sank.

'Go on.'

'I was working again the next day. Bríd told me when I came in that he'd been sleeping with my photo under his pillow. His behaviour was even more extreme. He never called me "Mammy" when any of the other children were around, but I could see it in his eyes. I'd been thinking about it all night, wondering what to do. When it was time to put him to bed, he asked me to read him a story – this was a first, too. When I finished, he looked at me, his eyes so wide, and said, in a tiny little voice: "Olly, wasn't I borned from you?"'

I looked at her, hoping she'd managed better this time. 'And?'

'I knew that saying the wrong thing might devastate him,' she said, her voice breaking, 'and he seemed so small and he needed me so much. I thought: "Is it so bad to pretend? He's such a lovely little boy really. Maybe he . . . maybe he *should* have been born from me. I mean, I'm like his mammy, aren't I? What did that bitch ever do for him other than treat him worse than an animal? At least I love him and mind him and am kind to him. Would it be wrong to say that he's mine?" I thought about that and I said: "Let's pretend for now that you *are* my baby," and I kissed him and turned out the light.'

I sighed and took out my cigarettes. Several things were running through my head, and none of them was very positive. I flipped open the top of the Zippo and struck the flint.

'Can I have one of those?' she asked, and I handed her the one I had just lit, taking another one for myself.

'The fact that you're as upset as you are, Olwyn, shows that you know that you could have handled yourself better,' I said, trying to keep my tone gentle; she was miserable enough without me giving her a tongue-lashing.

'Yeah,' she said. She had that awkward look people with cigarettes have when they don't usually smoke. She didn't seem to know what to do with it; how to hold it comfortably.

'Rule number one in childcare is never lie; always be honest. Playing games like you're doing, when the child is obviously insecurely attached to you, is just not right. There is no way it can end other than with Larry being hurt. And I can already see that you're hurting pretty badly too.'

She nodded.

'I wish I could tell you something different, but I'm

afraid that there's only one thing you can do, and that is go in there today and tell him the truth. You *aren't* his mother; he *wasn't* born of you. He already has a mother, and if he is to ever deal with all the shit that has happened to him, he's going to have to come to terms with who she is and the relationship he's had with her. Now, Olwyn, that's hard enough without you confusing the issue for him. I'm sorry, but there's no other way round this.'

She was crying again, but was nodding too. I wasn't telling her anything she didn't know; she just wanted confirmation from me, and possibly to confess to someone.

'I'm sorry,' she said.

'You don't need to apologize, Olwyn. We all mess up from time to time. My own career has had its share of disasters. You learn from them and make sure they don't happen again.'

'I . . . I actually liked the attention he gave me. It was lovely going in to work and having him waiting there, knowing that just seeing me was making his day. And I was proud of *myself*. Here I was, straight out of college, my first job, and *I'm* the one to tame the wild boy, the child no one else can handle. *I'm* the one he goes to. I thought I was doing so well. When we were working with him before, you, me and Karena, I felt so fucking useless. I thought that you both knew what you were doing, but I had nothing to contribute.'

'Olwyn, that probably had more to do with me than with you. I was worried about what you and Karena thought of my abilities. Instead of tending to your needs and thinking about how you both were feeling, I was concerned mostly with myself. I owe you an apology for that.'

She didn't seem to be listening to me.

'I was trying to be a good mother to him, you know. But I suppose that I don't really know what being a good parent is. My dad was never around, never available for any of us. My mam can be a bit scary. That's why I didn't want to meet you at home. She'd have gone mad if she thought that I'd messed up.'

'Parents can be a bit over-protective sometimes.'

'I wanted to be a mother for Larry.'

We were getting nowhere. Olwyn seemed to be falling deeper and deeper into an abyss that had been created a long time ago and which Larry had inadvertently uncovered.

'You aren't his mother, Olwyn. Sometimes what we do is like mothering – goddam it, they even call it "mothercare" in the college textbooks – but you have to make sure that neither the child, nor you, gets confused about it. That's part of the job.'

'I know,' she sobbed. 'But it's hard. When he said to me that I was his mother . . . for a moment, just a moment . . . I thought I was.'

I took her by the shoulders and turned her so that she was facing me. It was nearing eleven o'clock, and the sun was heating up the day. By lunchtime it would be uncomfortable. More people had arrived, the pathways becoming busier with teenagers on skateboards and women pushing children in prams. The park was full of the scent of blossoms and the sound of birdsong and insects buzzing about. It all seemed far away from us.

'Listen to me, Olwyn,' I said, looking her dead in the eye and speaking quietly but firmly. 'Every now and then you come across children who, for whatever reason, push your buttons. They make you crazy. When you encounter a child like that, you need to be able to identify it and *walk away*, because you can't help that child. All you're liable to do is mess him up further. I think that perhaps you have some stuff you need to work through, issues from your own childhood. That's nothing to be ashamed of, and it doesn't mean you're mad or an ineffectual childcare worker. But you *do* need to get some work done on it, or you're being irresponsible. I have some phone numbers I can give you – of good people. I can't set the counselling up for you, Olwyn. You have to do it yourself. Will you?'

She nodded.

'I can't be his key-worker any more, can I?'

'It would probably be better that you're not, but it's hard to call right now. We'll have to see how Larry responds.'

I paused, unsure how to frame what needed to be said next.

'People get into this work for lots of different reasons. Some people want to save the world. Some people like the power. Some people do it because they've been abused and want to make sure that it doesn't happen to the children on their watch. And some people do it because they never got the kind of love they deserved when they were little, and they have all this love inside them and they want to give it to children who were emotionally neglected, just like them.'

Olwyn laughed at that, but nodded. 'Yeah. That's about it.'

'There are far worse reasons for becoming a childcare worker,' I said.

She laid her head on my shoulder and said nothing. I sat with her in the noisy silence of the park for another forty-five minutes, and then dropped her to work. As she got out of the car, I said to her: 'You need to talk to Larry today, Olwyn.'

Her face was red from the crying, but she looked stronger than I had seen her before.

'I'll talk to him.'

'It's not all bad,' I told her. 'The fact that he's bonded to you so strongly shows that he's ready to ask for some help. That's really positive. This is by no means a wasted experience – it's up to all of us to capitalize on it. I'll stop by tomorrow and see how he's doing. It wouldn't be right for me to come in today and try to stir things up when he'll already be upset. I'll talk to Bríd and explain. Call me if you need to.'

'Thanks, Shane,' she said, and walked slowly up the path to the house.

It was almost dark when the girls appeared at their corner in the docklands. I had abandoned all sense of subtlety, and parked only a couple of yards up from their pitch as the shadows grew longer. They noticed me immediately but pretended not to. I turned on the light in my car and made as if to look for something in the glove compartment, giving them a few minutes to watch me from the corners of their eyes. What I really wanted was for Sylvie to have an opportunity to recognize me. Two middle-aged men turned the corner and walked past the group of young women. They were scruffy, dressed in dirty jeans and sweatshirts. The girls hailed them enthusiastically, but the men barely acknowledged them.

I got out of the Austin and approached the girls. My behaviour confused them. I was being too upfront. It was as if I didn't care if people saw me. They pretended to ignore me until I was upon them.

'Good evening, girls.'

''Lo.'

'Hiya, Mister.'

Sylvie was looking at me with a puzzled expression on her face. I didn't think she really knew who I was yet, but she seemed to have a vague memory and was struggling with it. I gestured towards her with a nod.

'I'd like a chat with this young lady, if I may.'

The heads of the other three turned to her. There was muttered conversation. They seemed to pick up on the fact that something was bothering her, and some hard looks were thrown my way. They could tell I wasn't a cop, but there are many worries for a streetwalker, people far worse than cops. I walked slowly to the car and leaned against it, waiting. I didn't want to scare them. Finally Sylvie separated herself from the group and came down the footpath. When she reached me she stood, trying to look brave and defiant. She was a fraction over five feet tall with short dark brown hair. I knew that her eyes were blue, but couldn't see them in the dark. Tonight she wore a black bra-top studded with fake diamonds and a short denim skirt. On her feet were white boots with high heels.

She was wearing no jewellery. In the glow of the halogen bulb she looked thin and pale. Her heavy make-up hid her age, but the frailness of a physique still very much in adolescence was obvious to anyone taking the time to look.

'Hello, Sylvie,' I said.

That stumped her.

'How do you know me?'

'You don't remember? I used to work in the care unit on Branch Street. It was a long time ago, but so far as I recall we were good friends.' I held my hand out to her. 'I'm Shane.'

Realization dawned slowly, and then recollection flooded back. It was joined by confusion and then anger. She thought I was cruising for tricks. My even being there was a betrayal, putting any good memories she had of me into a very different context. She didn't take my hand, just watched me with suspicion.

'Yeah, I remember you. You look older – you have a beard now. You only worked there for a while.'

'I was a student. I had to go back to college.'

'Huh, they all go sooner or later. It's no big deal.'

I said nothing to that. It is a fundamental truth of residential care that staff move on to other jobs, leaving children they may have worked with for years. As I had said to Olwyn earlier that day, childcare may seem like parenting, but it is, ultimately, a job. People who stick with it keep that clear in their heads. Those for whom it becomes personal end up doing something else before too long.

'So how've you been?' I asked, knowing as the nicety left my mouth that it was a terribly stupid thing to say.

'Oh, I've been great. Flyin' it.'

She was starting to lose interest now, wondering if I was there to indulge some tawdry fantasy and thinking that I might not have the guts to go through with it. I saw her casting looks back at her colleagues, who were watching us closely.

'Sylvie, will you come and have a cup of coffee with me? There's an all-night café around the corner.'

'The truck-stop. Yeah, I know it.'

She grinned lasciviously, and I understood how she knew it, but did not let myself linger on the thought.

'I just want to talk to you. Catch up.'

She shrugged and looked about her to see if a better offer was available, then returned her gaze to me. I saw something change in it. It was as if a mask had come down, a firewall.

'One hundred euro for half an hour, one eighty for an hour.'

I shook my head. 'No, I'm not hiring you. All I want is to have a cup of coffee and a chat.'

'Well I'm workin'. Take it or leave it. Of course,' she winked, 'if you pay me and you get bored of talkin', there's plenty else we can do.'

I sighed and shook my head. 'I'm not going to give you any money, Sylvie. I'll buy you a coffee – dinner, if you want – but I'm not going to rent you out. I know there are guys who look at you and see something they want, but what I see is that four-year-old I used to read *Cinderella* to. I'd like to get to know her again.'

She pouted. I couldn't tell whether it was real or put on.

'Don't you think I'm sexy?'

'No.'

'Don't you think I'm pretty?'

'You're a beautiful kid, but I'm too old for you, you're too young to be having sex and I don't think *anyone* should have to sell themselves. Put those three facts together and you've got one reason why there isn't going to be any money changing hands between us, Sylvie. Now,' I held out my arm to her, 'are we going to get something to eat or not?'

She paused, biting her lower lip in an expression of doubt which totally betrayed her age.

'Okay, but not for long. I'm supposed to work until midnight at least. If I'm gone and have nothin' to show for it, I'll get into trouble.'

She took my arm nervously, and together we walked up the street to the truck-stop. It was only a short stroll, but she spent the entire time looking about her, obviously wary of being seen.

The café was brightly lit and surprisingly clean. It smelt of fried food and freshly brewed coffee and had a black-and-white tiled floor with tables bolted to it, the seats all covered with red velour. It was busy, most of the booths occupied with dockworkers on their break or truckers just finished loading or unloading, stopping for some caffeine to fuel the run home. There was a pleasant buzz of men's voices. A waitress came and I asked for coffee. Sylvie enthusiastically ordered a cheeseburger, chips and a large chocolate milkshake. When the waitress had gone to get our order, I lit a cigarette, offering her the pack. She shook her head.

'So.' Suddenly I didn't know what to say. She looked terribly uncomfortable, not meeting my eyes and looking anywhere but at me. 'The last time I saw you, you were in res. I always thought you'd be fostered – there was a family interested in you, if I remember correctly. What happened?'

She shrugged and looked at the tabletop.

'God, Shane, that was years ago. I barely remember.'

'I know it was a long time ago. Ten years almost. But work with me, huh? What happened?'

She sighed, fiddling with a loose thread on her top.

'The family that were s'posed to take me, they wanted me because they couldn't have their own kids. Then the lady got pregnant. They didn't want me no more.'

It was a common enough story.

'Pity.'

'I didn't mind so much. I was happy in the Centre. They were real nice to me. I thought I'd be there for good.'

She fell silent. The waitress left cutlery on our table, and then came back with my coffee and Sylvie's milk-shake. Her eyes widened with pleasure at the sight of it.

'And?' I prompted her.

'And,' she took a long slurp of the shake, coming away from the glass with a thick brown moustache, 'my dad showed up.'

'Your dad?'

'He'd disappeared. When Mam ended up in the nut-house, they couldn't find him. But one day, when I was nine years old, he knocked on the door and asked to see me. I don't know how he tracked me down, but he did.'

'They didn't just hand you over . . .'

The food arrived. Sylvie picked up the ketchup bottle and began to douse her chips.

'No. They organized access visits. A worker came with me at first, to make sure he wasn't a psycho or nothin'. Then after a few months we were left mostly on our own, and in the end he would take me out for the whole day. He seemed real nice. He said that Mam had forced him to leave, that he had wanted to take me with him, but she wouldn't allow it. He told me he wanted us to be a family again, him and me.'

She began to cram the food into her mouth, eating as if her life depended on it.

'Good?' I asked.

'Mmm,' she nodded, giving me a ketchup-coated thumbs up.

'So I take it you were finally sent home with him?'

'Yeah, not long after my tenth birthday. They had a party for me at the Centre, cake and everythin'! And the next day he picked me up in a taxi and we went home. I was so happy. I'd been dreamin' about him comin' to get me since I was little, and here it was, happenin'. A dream come true. My fairy godmother had come through for me.'

I stubbed out my smoke in the small foil ashtray and lit another.

'How'd it work out?'

She laughed drily and picked up the burger.

'Shane, as soon as we got in the door of his flat, he handed me a mop and told me to get started, that I was his now and would have to work hard for my keep. You know, I didn't even mind. I wanted him to be happy, for me to be a good daughter. So I mopped, hoovered, dusted . . . I made his dinner that evenin'; and he never batted an eyelid, never said thanks. After we'd eaten, he told me he was goin' out and for me to go to bed. He told me if he came home and found me up, there'd be trouble.'

'So you went to bed?'

'Of course. I was a good little girl back then. It didn't help me though. Some time in the night I woke up and he was in bed with me. I didn't know what he was doin' at first, then I knew. Some of the other kids in the Centre had told me about it. I just never thought it would happen to me.'

'God, I'm sorry, sweetheart. Did it happen again after that?'

'Ooh.' She wiped her mouth and sat back, belching loudly. 'Most nights for the first year. If I was lucky, he rode me and then fell asleep. If I wasn't, he'd give me a hidin' afterwards. Not the face, nowhere bruises would be seen. Social workers visited the odd time, but, fuckin' eejit that I was, I thought he was testin' me, that he wanted to see how much I loved him, how much I could take, so I smiled and put tissue paper down me knickers to stop the blood comin' out me arse and told them everything was fantastic.'

'They didn't notice anything?'

'Don't be a moron. How could they? He'd fooled me, fooled everyone. Of course they didn't.'

'Did you run away?'

'Where the fuck to? He found me in the Centre after

five years of bein' away – he'd find me again. I'm still with him. Sure, he's the one that sends me out.'

I nodded slowly and motioned for more coffee.

'Would you like some dessert?'

'No, ta,' she said, standing up. 'It was nice catchin' up with you, but I've to get back. If me da finds out I was slackin', he'll fuckin' kill me.'

'Sylvie, wait,' I said, catching her arm gently. 'You can't leave like this. I want to help you.'

She smiled and firmly removed my hand.

'I knew it. Is this how you get your kicks? Want to take me home as your little sex-slave? I don't work like that.'

'No! I told you that isn't what I'm about. You shouldn't be living like this. There's a guy I work with – he can help me to organize somewhere for you to stay. Don't worry about your father. You'll be safe. There's a place I know, a residential setting; they have plenty of extra space and they're good people.'

She sat down again and took my hand. She was looking at me as if I was the child and she the adult.

'Shane, I've been in res. It didn't make any fuckin' difference to my life. Look at me now. I'm a whore, Shane. My da is my pimp. This is what I am, and this is where I'm stayin'. There's no point in my goin' anywhere with you. He'll come and get me and no one will be able to stop him and it'll be worse than before. Thanks, really. You're sweet, but I have to go now.'

She smiled and stood up and then leaned over and kissed me on the cheek. Her eyes were wet, but she wiped at them roughly and walked quickly to the door. I felt awful. This was not the way it was supposed to happen.

116

She should have been reluctant at first, but then seen that I was right and gone with me gratefully. That was how it had played out in my head. I watched her go out the door, then I dropped some money on the table and took off after her.

She was ten yards up the street, and I called after her: 'Sylvie, I'm sorry, but you're coming with me. You're a kid, and I'm an adult, and this is my job.'

'Fuck off, Shane, will you? I'm runnin' out of patience.'

I took her arm, more firmly this time.

'I mean it, Sylvie. I'm not leaving you here, and that's the end of it. I'd be a pretty lousy person if I did. Now come on.'

She shook her head, scowling, and began to shout.

'Help! Help me! He's attackin' me! Rape!' Her cries were piercing. For a little girl, she had quite a vocal range.

'Sylvie,' I said, looking about in embarrassment and starting to walk her briskly towards the car. 'Stop it.'

'Help me, somebody!' she screamed, trying to pull away from me.

Her exclamations had attracted attention: three men who had just come out of the truck-stop ran up to us.

'Hey, fella, the little lady doesn't seem to want to go with you,' one said. He was taller than me by a head and weighed around fourteen kilos more, a pendulous belly hanging low over his belt, arms like pistons.

'Help me, mister. I don't know this fella and he says he's takin' me to his car.'

'I think you should let her go, bud,' another of the men said, laying his hand on my shoulder and squeezing. He was smaller than his cohort, but still bigger than me, muscles showing in bunches under his dirty white T-shirt. A needle of pain shot down my arm.

'If you would just let me explain,' I gasped, involuntarily letting Sylvie go.

She took off like a shot, running down the street without looking back. I made to follow, but the three Good Samaritans pinned me to the wall.

'You fucking idiots,' I grunted, struggling against them. 'Let me go. You don't understand –'

A punch was delivered to my stomach that took all my breath away. I sagged to the ground.

'Fuckin' pervert,' one of them muttered, and kicked me in the gut.

I heard footsteps moving away, but was in no condition to follow or respond. I had failed Sylvie again. I lay there until I was able to breathe properly, and then lay there some more. Getting up seemed a waste of effort.

7

It was as if I had stepped into a British situation comedy – *The Good Life*, or maybe *Keeping Up Appearances*. Molly Henry was pouring tea from a bone-china pot into a little cup that was sitting in an exquisite saucer. She was immaculately dressed in a silk, floral ensemble, which matched her shoes perfectly. The room was surgically clean and smelt of expensive furniture polish and carpet shampoo. It appeared that Molly (or maybe the help – I hadn't seen any, but I always assumed they were discreetly hidden away somewhere) had gone on an epic cleaning spree. I felt out of place: uncouth and somehow too big for the environment, like Gulliver just having landed in Lilliput.

'Cream and sugar? Or would you prefer lemon?'

'No, thank you. Black is fine.'

Molly handed me the cup and saucer and sat down on an armchair.

'I'm so sorry that Mina won't see you. She won't talk to anyone, at present.'

'Is she here? I thought she'd be at the workshop.'

'No, we've decided that she won't be going to that awful place any more.'

That perplexed me.

'Can I ask you why?'

'Well, she's not safe there, is she?'

'That can be easily rectified. Just let the staff know she needs to be watched. In fact, you probably don't have to tell them now. They've been made painfully aware of it.'

'No, we have decided. She'll remain at home where we can care for her properly. We may employ a tutor.'

'And her social needs? How will you cater for those? Will you employ some young people for her to be friends with?'

'She has her club.'

'And she'll be safer there than at work?'

'Dirk or myself will accompany her.'

I put the cup and saucer down on a marble coaster on the coffee table. I was afraid that I would drop them.

'Mina is a bright, vital, lovely young woman,' I said. 'She needs to have some freedom, an outlet, something that is just hers and doesn't involve you or Dirk. She loves you and respects you, but I think that you may be smothering her. I'm not a big fan of the workshop system, but at least she was out of the house and mixing with her peers. Don't cut off one of the few lifelines she has.'

Molly Henry smiled sweetly at me. 'It was so good of you to bring her home to us. We're very grateful.'

'Molly, did you hear a single thing I just said?'

'Of course, but our minds are quite made up. She will remain at home.'

I sighed.

'Is it all right if I try to speak to Mina? Seeing as I'm here, I should probably give it a go.'

'Certainly. Come with me, please.'

She led me into the hallway and up an ornate flight of stairs to a landing. She knocked at a mahogany door.

'Mina, darling, Shane is here. He wonders if he might speak with you.'

There was no sound.

'Mina, are you awake?'

'Go away!' The two words were shouted with vehemence.

'I'm sorry, Shane,' Molly said.

'Can I stay here for a few minutes anyway?'

The woman looked puzzled. 'Why?'

'I'd like to sit here on the landing and talk to Mina. She doesn't need to answer me, but I know she'll hear, even if she doesn't listen.'

Molly shrugged. 'If that's what you want.'

She turned and walked back down the stairs. I sat on the carpeted floor, leaning my back against the door.

'Mina, I'm just going to hang out with you for a bit. There are a few things I'd like to speak about. You don't have to say anything if you don't want to. Okay?'

Silence.

'I know you're feeling a lot of different things at the moment. Maybe so many emotions are running through you that they're hard to tell apart. I guess you're probably angry with me for interfering in your business; embarrassed at me finding you doing the things you were doing; afraid of what's going to happen next; sad at having hurt your parents' feelings. It's all confusing and frightening, one big problem. But know this: *it isn't a problem we can't solve*. Your folks care a lot about you, the people at the workshop are your friends, I want to help you as much as I can, and you are a person with a lot of skills and abilities. Now, the way I see it, taking all those facts into consideration, there are more positives in the equation than negatives. If we all put our heads together, we can find a solution. What do you say?'

No response.

'The most important person in all this is you, Mina. Everyone wants what's best for you, though it may be hard for you to see that just now. Your mum and dad have decided that you aren't going to the workshop any more. Did they tell you?'

Nothing.

'They want to pay somebody to come in and teach you. Your mother says that she's going to start going to the Abled-Disabled Club with you too. Won't that be fun? Going to see your friends with Mum waiting around to see what you're getting up to. I know I wouldn't like it. But you know what? I can understand why they're doing it. You see, they don't know what's going on in your head, so they're grasping at straws to try and figure it out. You're not giving them many options.'

Dead air.

'Mina, I'm on your side. Fuck it, I'm on everyone's side, but my main job is to be here for you. I was never sent out here to control you, like you thought. I was sent to be your friend, to try and see things from your point of view and to help your parents see things that way too. Now, I can't do that unless you talk to me and tell me what your point of view is.'

Emptiness.

'I can wait, Mina. I'm a patient guy, and I'm not going to stop working with you – working *for* you, just because you take to your room and throw a strop. When you're feeling up to it, we'll talk. Whatever's going on, we can work it out. I promise.'

Mina didn't respond. Molly didn't rush upstairs to tell me how inspiring my words had been. The key to the whole awful mess didn't drop out of the ether into my lap. I sat in the quiet house on one side of the door, the girl on the other, her mother somewhere below, each of us alone with our thoughts.

Ellen, the woman who ran Mina's section at the workshop, didn't much want to speak to me either. I met her that lunchtime in their canteen. Molly had neglected to explain to the management that her daughter would no longer be attending, and had given me permission to fill them in on what had happened. Ellen was friendly and polite, but I could tell that the whole thing was making her uncomfortable. I drank some truly foul coffee, tried to eat a tasteless chicken salad sandwich, and listened as she danced around the reasons why Mina may have gone to The Sailing Cot, speaking for a full five minutes without telling me anything.

'People with special needs sometimes see things differently than the rest of us do, and are driven by impulses that aren't always obvious. You have to take that into consideration and not draw any rash conclusions.'

'I haven't drawn any conclusions. I haven't a clue what's going on.'

'Well, that's probably for the best.'

I admitted defeat with the sandwich and dropped it back onto the cardboard plate.

'How, precisely, is it for the best? Mina is in pain, Ellen.

She's involved in something that's out of her control, and we, as the carers, have a responsibility to help her deal with it. I don't know whether she was with that man of her own free will or not. Until I do know, I can't really move forward, do you understand?'

Ellen coughed and looked unhappy. 'Well, I mean to say, she couldn't have been with him because she wanted to be.'

'Stranger things have happened.'

'No . . . but . . . you see, people like Mina . . . they don't *do* that kind of thing.'

'What?'

'Mina is still a child, Shane, in most senses of the word.'

'I take it that you don't endorse relationships of a . . . er . . . physical nature between people with intellectual disabilities then?'

'For the love of God, they don't know what they're getting into! It's difficult enough for people with all their faculties to make informed choices about sexual issues without inflicting that kind of thing on people with special needs. No, we don't encourage it at all.'

'But these are *adults*, Ellen.'

'No, Shane, they're not. Chronologically, perhaps, but intellectually and emotionally – in the ways that count – they are very much children. How do you explain about venereal diseases to someone who still likes to watch *The Tweenies*? Tell me where you'd begin a discussion about different types of contraception and the moral implications – most of our clients are from Catholic families. If relationships were permitted, you would have to accept that children might result. Could you, in all good conscience, allow someone who needs assistance to tie her shoelaces bring a child into the world? Or would you simply sterilize all the females? This is a huge, murky field, Shane, and I think it is wise to draw clear boundaries.'

'Is it not better', I said, choosing my words carefully and trying not to get angry, 'to take each case on its own merits and not write off a hugely important part of human experience for a whole section of the population? How would you feel if you were, without any recourse, sentenced to a life of celibacy?'

'You're deflecting. I don't have a disability.'

'Sex is not just about fucking, Ellen. It's about intimacy and human contact and fulfilment and self-affirmation. It's an expression of who we are. It's psychologically and sociologically important. Some would say that it's a basic human right.'

'I think that's nonsense. You sound like you've been reading too many women's magazines.'

'Who's deflecting now?'

'Look, Shane, these are my last words on this topic: yes, it does happen to be my personal opinion that sexual contact should not be permitted between people with learning disabilities, but it is also the policy of the work-shop. We believe that it would be detrimental to the community here if the trainees were distracted from their learning and their work by such trivialities.'

'There's not much more to say then, is there?'

'No. There isn't.'

I went out to my car in a lousy mood. I had spent an entire morning trying to make some sense of Mina's case, and was no closer than I had been when I started.

It seemed that the more people I tried to talk to, the fewer people wanted to talk to *me*. Mina didn't want to discuss things, Molly and Dirk were tight-lipped, and now the workshop had closed ranks too. I lit a cigarette and turned on the ignition. I decided that I needed some music and took out my box of tapes. I settled on a collection by Neil Young and was putting it in the stereo when I noticed a young man standing just inside the door of the main building, watching me closely. He was short and broad, with a head of light-brown curls. He wore a brightly coloured knitted jumper and ill-fitting blue jeans. A trainee, I guessed. Neil had started singing: *When you were young and on your own; how did it feel to be alone?* I looked back at my observer. Did he want to speak to me? I was about to roll down the window and call him over, but he suddenly ducked back inside. Shrugging, I released the hand-brake and moved off. *But only love can break your heart; try to be sure right from the start.* As I turned out the gate, I spotted him again, from the corner of my eye, still watching me from one of the windows of the front hall. I wondered briefly who he was and what he wanted, but then I was down the street and my mind had turned to the Walshes and I didn't think about him again for several weeks.

Micky, Bobby and I were singing along with the TV.

'What's the story in Balamory, wouldn't you like to know?'

I should have felt like an idiot, but when you're with kids and there aren't any other adults around, inhibitions tend to go out the window. I'm not a regular viewer of

Balamory, but there are worse children's shows on television (I don't much like *Barney*, and I'm not ashamed to admit that the *Teletubbies* freak me out). When I arrived at the house that afternoon, Biddy met me at the door. She'd had visitors the day before, and the boys had not got to bed until late. They were a bit tired, she told me, and probably wouldn't be up for much. I went into the living room and found Bobby and Micky sprawled on the couch in front of the box. They said hi, but, despite my best efforts, could not work up any enthusiasm for play. I decided to let it go for one day and to just spend some time with them watching the television. It might, I surmised, even give us some topics for discussion. Children's programmes tend to be thematic, covering a particular subject or trying to articulate a specific lesson. We didn't have to watch passively. So I surreptitiously tried to turn the experience into a play activity, singing along, pointing out things on the screen (colours, numbers, letters), talking back to the characters and making it as interactive as possible. The boys responded positively, and we had a pretty good time.

'Would you like a cup of tea?' Biddy stuck her head in the door, obviously picking up that the session was much less structured today.

'No, thanks,' I said, and with a loud pop that caused us all to jump the television went dead.

The boys groaned.

'Oh no, it's brokeded,' Micky said, scuttling over and switching it on and off.

Bobby remained on the couch, but was pointing the remote control and pressing all the buttons in the vain hope that this might help. Without the glow from the screen, the living room suddenly seemed very gloomy and oppressive. I shivered. It was cold. I hadn't noticed before. I reached up and flicked the light switch. Nothing.

'It's not the TV,' I said. 'It's the power.'

I pulled back one of the curtains and could see the flickering of a TV screen through the front window of the house across the road. It was just us, then. The boys were still gazing at the screen as if they expected it to spring into life at any moment.

'I paid the bill.' Biddy was pacing. She seemed distressed.

'It's probably just a fuse,' I said. 'Or maybe something's caused the trip-switch to go. The wiring's quite old in these houses, isn't it?'

Biddy didn't respond, just continued her frenzied pacing.

'Do you know how to change a fuse, Biddy?'

'Toddy did all that stuff,' she said shakily, her voice full of tears.

That was probably why she was so bothered. She had never before had to cope with minor household malfunctions. At that moment it occurred to me that I couldn't see if she was crying or not. It didn't make sense, but the room actually seemed to be getting darker. I looked at my watch. The luminous hands told me it was four thirty in the afternoon. We were in the middle of summer; the sun was blazing outside. So why was my breath coming out in clouds and why could I barely see Biddy's face?

'Where's the fuse box?'

A blank look.

'I'll have a scout around,' I said. 'It's probably in the utility room.'

It was, just above the back door. The room, which was situated at the rear of the house, contained a washing machine and a small sink unit. It was long and narrow, and was accessed from a door off the kitchen. A small window looked out onto the back garden. I pulled over a stool and climbed up onto it. The main fuse had blown completely – it was black and smouldering, some of the coils glowing red in the half-light. I hopped down, got a tea towel from the kitchen and used it to unscrew the fitting; it was too hot to touch. Branches scraped at the window outside, making a sound like a wild animal trying to get in. It was an urgent sound, and set my teeth on edge. It seemed to get inside my head, pins and needles in my brain. I set the half-melted fuse aside and looked at the spares that were lying in the tray. I had to strike the flame on my lighter so that I could see what I was doing. Then I spotted the one I was looking for. I picked it up and heard the door of the utility room close behind me.

'Biddy, is that you?'

Footsteps tapped across the tiled floor. I remember noting that the stride seemed to be too long to be Biddy's and then the stool was wrenched from under me. I toppled backwards and landed with all my weight on the back of my head. Light exploded before my eyes and the scraping at the window became almost deafening, enfolding me until that was all there was. The last thought that flickered across my consciousness before I passed out was that I couldn't be hearing branches – the trees and bushes were at the other end of the garden, at the ditch.

Throbbing pain was the first thing I became aware of, then the dim play of light and shadow across my eyelids, as if people were moving about above me. I forced my eyes open and sat up shakily. I was alone. The scratching had stopped; the stool was lying on its side at my feet. Holding my head gingerly, I went to the door and turned the handle. It was locked. For a second I panicked, pushing and pulling with all my might.

'Biddy!' I shouted, and immediately regretted it because my headache increased.

I took out my mobile phone, but there was no signal. I switched it off, then on again. There had to be a signal – there was *always* a signal here. After two failed attempts, I gave up and banged loudly on the wood with my fist. Despite myself, I began to get worried. What had just happened to me? What was going on in this house? I have always been a rational person, naturally sceptical about anything beyond the realms of science, but trapped in a tiny room in a haunted house in one of the most violent parts of the city, I found my intellectual resolve weakening.

Finally I heard footsteps and voices. The handle turned, the door was tested and then a key scraped in the lock. It was Biddy, looking puzzled, the two boys peering around her legs.

'No luck, then?' she asked uncertainly. 'How'd you lock yourself in?'

'Very funny,' I said petulantly, feeling really angry. 'You can change the fuse yourself, or get a neighbour to do it. I don't care. I'm not here to be a punchbag.'

'What are you goin' on about? Why didn't you try the back door?'

She seemed to be genuinely confused.

I went to the door leading to the back garden. The handle turned smoothly and it swung open. In exasperation, I realized that I could have got out this way at any time. I stood, blinking in the sunlight, basking in the heat of the evening. I could feel the cold seeping from the open doorway. I looked at the small utility-room window. I had been right – there were no branches anywhere near it. Something snapped in me momentarily, and I found that I couldn't move. My mind just stalled.

'Shane, are you okay?'

Bobby's voice wrenched me back to awareness.

'Yeah, Bob, I'm fine.'

'Are you goin' to fix the telly?'

'Yeah. Of course I will.'

I put in the new fuse, making Biddy hold the stool and feeling like a complete sissy for asking her to do it. The television blared back into life, light bulbs hummed and the shadows fled back to their lairs. I sank down onto the couch between the boys and accepted a bag of frozen peas to apply to my head. As the kids watched *Power Rangers*, I quietly told Biddy what had happened. They had been in the living room all the time, she said when she'd heard my story, waiting for the television to come back on. I must have over-balanced and the door slammed shut, blown by a freak breeze with enough force to cause it to jam. Yes, I agreed. It had to be that.

The boys made no comment. They had, in fact, gone very quiet.

8

The grounds around Rivendell spread over more than an acre. In the middle of the nineteenth century they had been planted with many different species of trees, shrubs and flowers, which the nuns tended with devotion. When the sisters moved on to other pastures, the Health Executive employed a gardener to come in and work one afternoon a week on the rambling garden. It simply wasn't enough; the area in front of the house, which could be seen from the road, was given priority, the rest was left to its own devices. The place gradually became a jungle.

The children who called Rivendell home played on the well-kept lawns, which had some swings, a slide, a climbing frame and goalposts for soccer. All the children, that was, except the Byrnes. The twins, as if by an inner voice, were drawn to the thickets, the wooded areas and the dense foliage of the abandoned garden at the rear of the old house. It offered them a haven, a primordial landscape within which they were far better equipped than the rest of us. They could climb trees with an agility that was almost simian. Low to the ground, they moved remarkably quickly on all fours. Once Larry and Francey disappeared into the undergrowth, they came out only when they wanted to. It was a testament to the work the staff team had done that they had ever come out at all.

Bríd stood with me at the edge of the wood.

'Olwyn spoke to Larry,' she said. 'She was very nice, but she said that they couldn't pretend any more. She was his friend, and she cared for him, but that was all.'

'How'd he take it?'

'Very well, we thought. He went quiet, seemed a bit subdued, but we weren't going to complain about that. Olwyn tried to engage him; he wasn't interested. He hasn't spoken to her since. Then, last night, when we went out for a game of football after supper, he and Francey took off into the trees as they always do. We didn't give it another thought until we called them to come in for bed. Francey came. Larry didn't.'

'Did she tell you where he was?'

'Oh yes. She said that Larry was sad, and would be staying outside. He didn't want to be with the rest of us. Wanted to be on his own. I called for him again, told him to pack in the nonsense and come inside, but he stayed good to his word.'

'Did anyone go in there after him?'

'Yes, Olwyn and I went, once we'd put the others to bed. We spent hours roaming around, and one of the night staff stayed on the lawn on a garden chair until morning, in case he decided to show his face, but there was no such luck.'

'How do you know he's in there? He might have run off.'

'Oh, we've heard him. He's been shouting and wailing sporadically. Animal sounds, mostly; but it's him.'

'Keening.'

'What?'

'He's grieving. He's lost his mother all over again.'

'Perhaps. Or he could just want to lead us on another merry dance. I thought all his sedate behaviour was too good to be true.'

'Such cynicism in one so young,' I sighed. I often wondered why Bríd had ever become involved in child-care. She certainly didn't seem to like children. 'Well,' I had put it off for long enough, 'I suppose I'd better see if I can find him.'

'Good luck. You're wasting your time of course. He won't come until he feels like it.'

'Well, maybe he's ready.'

Bríd guffawed loudly and turned back to the house.

'Don't get lost in there, or fall and break your ankle. I don't want to have to send out a search party looking for *you* as well.'

'I'll try,' I said as sweetly as I could, and ducked into the shadow of the trees.

Under the boughs of spruce and ash that were planted on the edge of the wild area, it was cool and pleasant. There was a gentle breeze that morning, and it moved the branches languidly, creating a sound like whispering. I walked in a straight line for about five minutes; the branches created a ceiling overhead, so there were few ground plants, and at first the going was easy. I came to a fallen tree that lay like a dead serpent across the path. Something moved in a thicket to my left, a quick burst of noise. I stopped dead.

'Larry?' I called. 'It's Shane.'

If it was him, he didn't want to talk – the noise moved steadily away. I went to go in the same direction, but saw that the copse was mostly bramble. I decided that it might be more sensible to go around rather than through.

As I travelled deeper into the scrub, the terrain became more difficult to navigate. The trees cleared slightly, and I found myself wading through high grass and nettles. After receiving several stings, I doubled back and broke a sturdy limb from an alder to use as a machete, and returned, cutting a wider path for myself. As the sun rose higher and the day became hotter, swarms of midges rose from the earth about me. At first, I beat them off with my hands, but before long they were crawling all over me, getting into my eyes, up my nose, in my mouth. Just as I was about to give in, the grass ended and I was standing on the cracked paving of a narrow, ornamental path overlooking a pond blanketed in some kind of yellow algae. The water was still and gave off the aroma of stagnancy. In the middle was what seemed to be a small island, covered with thick trees and vines. The scum was parted in one spot, where something had made a path through the dank water to the centre.

'Larry, come on. I know you're over there.'

I stood quietly and listened. Birdsong; the wind in the grass behind me; the ambient hum of the midges and dragonflies flitting above the surface of the mere.

'Okay, I'm coming over,' I shouted, 'but I'm pissed off about getting into this water. It doesn't look healthy.'

I climbed down from the bank into the stale, slimy pool. The bottom felt slippery under my boots, and I stopped to steady myself, leaning heavily on the stick. Submerging was most certainly not part of my plan. I took wide sloshing steps. The temperature of the water was disturbingly warm. I fancied that I could hear the bacteria breeding in it. After much cursing and several near duckings, I pulled myself up onto the bank of the island. In disgust, I noted that the algae had clung to my jeans in a foul outer layer, like a custard-skin.

I sat for a few moments to get my breath back, and then turned to examine the island's interior. What I saw was a solid wall of trees. It appeared to be impenetrable.

'Larry, come on out, will you?'

I began to pick my way along the perimeter of the dense grove. The island proved to be bigger than I had at first thought; the pond was actually a small lake, longer than it was wide. More than once the ground became too narrow for me, and I had to step back into the water. Finally I found an opening. It may have been a path created by animals, or it could have been planted that way purposely; in any case it was essentially a corridor of tall conifers. On each side the trees formed an impregnable barrier, so there was only the way ahead or back. It had become very quiet. Above me the needled branches obscured the sky, the pathway dark and close with the damp smell of earth and the sharper aroma of wood-sap.

I became aware of movement. At first, I thought I was imagining things. It seemed to happen only when I was moving, stopping when I did, but after several minutes I was certain. I was being shadowed. Using my peripheral vision, I looked left and right, but could see only the dense trunks. Casting my eyes above, I saw that there was no way even Larry could move through the foliage of the canopy – it was too thick and treacherous. That left one place he could be.

Without warning I dropped to the ground, falling flat so that I could see the narrow area between the lowest branches of the trees and the forest floor. Despite being prepared for what I saw, I still had to stifle a yell of surprise.

There, gazing back at me from the shadowy seam, was a face, yellow and wide-eyed. The child was spread-eagled, almost touching the ground, elbows bent, fingers clutching the earth, ready to scuttle away into the darkness in a second if such action was needed. Like a cat, it hissed at me, raising a clawed hand in warning.

'Larry, cool it, okay? I don't mean any harm.'

'I amn't no boy!'

Slowly, as my eyes grew accustomed to the dimness, I saw long hair plastered down the slender back. I was looking at Francey Byrne!

'I'm sorry, honey,' I said quietly, keeping my voice low and my hands open, where she could see them. 'I wasn't expecting you, and you're all wet and covered in that yellow stuff from the lake.'

'*I amn't no boy!*'

'Why are you following me?'

Francey's eyes narrowed as she considered the question.

'I wanted to see what you was doin out'n here. See if you could get about wit'out hurtin' yoursel'. Them two last night, they was all scairt an' fallin' over and jumpin' up an' down ev'ry time the wind blewed.'

'How'd I do?'

'You sounds liken a big monster stumpin' 'bout. I hears you breathin' from a good bit 'way, don't hardly need t' see ya.'

I grinned. 'Did I hear *you* back near the house?'

'I letted you. Wanted to see how you liked takin' a swim.'

'You wanted me to come this way?'

She nodded, a small smile playing about her lips.

'Why?'

Using only her hands to drag herself, leaving her legs straight out behind her as rudders, she crawled with unnerving speed towards me. I stood up quickly, not wanting her to catch me on the ground. She seemed to flow into a standing position, her head low and her hair hanging over her face. I saw that she was wearing only a grimy white T-shirt hanging to her knees. No shoes. Slowly, she raised her head to look at me between the strands of wet, filthy hair. I moved my feet apart, got balanced, expecting her to spring at me.

'Larry is near here,' she said finally. 'This be where he comes.'

I hadn't expected that.

'Do you want me to find him?'

Francey shrugged. 'He does be sad.' She seemed to be thinking, as if the conversation we were having was completely new ground for her. 'Why he be so sad?'

I took a step towards her, squatting down so that I was at her eye level.

'Why do you think he's sad, Francey?'

She was gazing into the trees, and I sensed that she was fighting an urgent need to spring into one and get away from me. Love for her brother and an understanding that he was unhappy were all that was keeping her where she was.

'I don't know. He been actin' weird.'

'Has he?'

'Yeah, liken a baby or sumpin'. I don' like it so much when he be like dat. I want him to be liken the old Larry again.' She looked at me, an open plea on her face. 'You help him, okay? You make him right again. I'm lonely in this ol' place wit'out him. Them other kids, they don' like me none, an' I don' like them. I like my brudder. You make him be happy again, okay?'

I stood up, my knees popping.

'I can't promise that I'll make Larry any happier, Francey, but I'm going to see if I can't at least get him to go back to the house. It's not so easy to make someone be happy if they're not. I think that his feelings are hurt, and that's why he's hiding out here.'

'No! You tell me you'll make my brudder happy or I'ma not show you where he be's.'

'Francey, I won't lie to you – not now, not ever. I can't wave a magic wand, or say a spell and make things right. If I could, I'd fix it that all the bad stuff that happened to you and your brother never did. What I *can* do is be your friend, and help you to talk about things that are on your mind. That sometimes makes you feel a bit better, to let that stuff out. Now, maybe Larry will feel like talking when we go to see him, or maybe he won't. I can't make him talk, and neither can you.'

'If'n I tells him to talk to you, he will.'

'It doesn't work that way, Francey.'

She scowled. 'Come on. I'll show ya.'

I heard him before I saw him. A wail that sounded more animal than person rose above the tree line, the sound of

140

abject misery. Francey stopped dead and waited for it to die out, eyes closed, head to one side.

'He used to make them howls when we was locked up. He never done it since they took us out. I can't get why he be doin' it again. He isn't locked up no more.'

'There's lots of reasons to be unhappy.'

'They don' even beat on us,' she said, opening her eyes and staring at me. 'We's done everyt'in' we can dream up, and they don' hit us or kick us or take a strap to us neither.'

'No one will hurt you here, Francey. At least, not like that. There'll be no more beatings.'

'I don' understand this place.' She moved forward a few more paces, and stopped at a rhododendron bush, heavy with scent. 'T'rough here.'

Behind the bush a narrow stream was flowing, a log acting as a bridge across it. Beyond was a wide clear spot on the bank of the island, and Larry was sitting there with his back to me, looking out over the water. I called to him, not wanting to startle the boy.

'I ain't goin' back,' he said, his gaze remaining on the lake.

I walked over, Francey hanging back, seemingly torn between giving us some privacy and hearing what was said.

'I haven't come to take you anywhere. I just want to talk.'

'How'd you find me?'

'I think you know.'

'Francey.'

I said nothing, waiting to see what his response to the

betrayal would be. Slowly his head turned to look at me. I could sense Francey behind. His eyes travelled to where his twin was hovering by the stream, and lingered on her for a moment. His focus returned to the water without comment.

'You go on back now. Tell 'em . . . tell 'em I'm a gone.'

I sat on the wet bank next to him. I was filthy and sopping anway.

'They know you haven't gone anywhere, Larry. They can hear you crying back at the house.'

'I's not cryin'. That's singin'.'

'Well it's the saddest song I've ever heard. I'm sorry about what happened with Olwyn. She really cares about you; it's just that she can't lie to you and pretend to be your mother. It's not right for her to do that.'

'I don' know what you're talkin' 'bout. I was only messin' wit' dat girl. I lovens my mam. She was rale daycent to me.'

'I'm sure your mother loved you, but she didn't always treat you very well. That's why you're here.'

'You fuck off talkin' 'bout my mam! You don't know nu'in 'bout her *or* 'bout me.'

'I know enough to know that you had a rough time at home. I've seen the scars on you and the sadness and pain in your eyes. I've been doing this sort of work for a long time, and I know what that means. You're right, I don't know your mother. I've never met her, or your dad for that matter. They might be good people. But what they *did*, to you and your sister, that wasn't good.'

'I shouldn' be in dis here place. Me 'n' Francey, we were rale happy at home. We used sleep at night in a grand bed wit' clayne sheets on it and I had a great, big brown teddy bear wit a red an' white bow tie. He was all fluffy an' warm. My mam used make us hot milk on the stove in a burner so's we'd sleep, and Dad would tell us bedtime stories, 'bout dragons 'n' princes 'n' dwarfs 'n' such. I 'member one time he bringed home a tub o' ice-cream for us and set it down on the table and we eated it all up. He was a great dad.'

I looked back at Francey, who was staring at her brother open-mouthed.

It was quite possible that some of what he was saying was true: it is rare, even in extreme cases, for there to be no gentle and compassionate interactions between parent and child. Mr and Mrs Byrne may well have been kind to the twins at times. Judging from Francey's expression, however, it seemed that her memories differed considerably from her brother's.

'I'm glad that you have such good things to say about your mother and father,' I said. 'And those things will always be with you. Treasure them. But it doesn't take away from the fact that you just couldn't stay living at home. Your parents were hurting you too much, and you weren't getting enough to eat. Your father and mother need some help with that.'

'It's all cack, what you's sayin',' Larry said, almost in a whisper. 'My daddy is a great fella. Peoples is jealous of 'im, s'all. They's told lies about him and Mam, that's why me 'n' Francey has to be here. Mam and Dad'll sort it ou' then we's goin' back, see? I know that. You jus' wait 'n' see.'

'You know, Larry, there's always hope that you and

Francey can go back home. But the only way that'll happen is if your mum and dad get a lot of help. It might take a long time. I don't know if they're even talking to the social workers about it. I'll check it out for you.'

'You do what'n'ever you likes to do. I *know* I'm goin' home. Soon.'

I looked back at Francey. She was watching us both silently, tears streaming down her face, tiny rivers running through the yellow algae that was caked on her thin cheeks.

I stayed with them on the island until the sun started to dip in the sky, and midges descended on the ochre surface of the lake in a foul cloud. Then I took them both by the hand, and we walked slowly back to the house.

I hadn't been back to the residential unit where I'd first met Sylvie since I had been in college. It was a small house on a pleasant street in a good part of town. The manager let me in and brought me into the tiny front office. I didn't know him. All the staff who worked with me had long since moved on.

'So you were here when?'

'Close to ten years ago. I came as part of a college placement, but I was asked to stay on and do some relief work. I'm sure you'll find records of me on file.'

He sighed deeply and went to a bright green filing cabinet. He was a short, portly, bearded man, his receding hair gelled back and tied in a stubby ponytail. He wore his trousers high at the waist with the belt chinked tight, so his round belly seemed to be divided in two, a bulge on either side of the leather band.

'And you want to know about young Sylvie Lambe?'

'Yes. I work for the Dunleavy Trust now. She came up in connection with another case. I'm trying to trace her.'

He continued to riffle through the files, his back to me.

'Got any ID?'

I walked around so I could place the card in his line of vision. He acknowledged it with a nod, pulling a tattered file, putting it on top of the cabinet and then opening a lower drawer and squatting stiffly to look in there. Seconds later: 'Yeah, here we go.'

He heaved himself up and brought the two files to the desk, motioning for me to sit.

'Well, you check out. You were here for a few months. Pace too slow for you?'

'I liked it here fine. No one offered me a full-time job.'

He shrugged and picked up the second file.

'What do you want to know about Sylvie?'

'The address she moved to when she left here, and anything you can give me on her father.'

He put his short legs up on the desk. He was wearing cherry-coloured cowboy boots with very high heels.

'I've got an address here for a flat on the other side of the river. I'll copy it for you. As for her old man, one Joseph Lambe – there's a ream of reports on access visits, case conferences, psychological evaluations, all the usual stuff.'

'Can I get copies?'

'Look, there's a photocopier in the hall. Why don't you run off the whole file?'

'Thanks.'

'Well, we have to look after our own, don't we?' I couldn't work out whether he was being sarcastic or not, but decided it didn't matter.

He took a pack of long, thin, brown cigarettes from his breast pocket and lit one with a small gold lighter.

'What's your interest here – *really*?'

'She's not doing so well.'

He blew a cloud of menthol smoke at me. 'So things didn't work out in the long run. Sometimes they don't.'

'They didn't even work out in the short run. He started abusing her the very first night she stayed with him, and then put her out on the game.'

'And how does she fall under your jurisdiction? We haven't received any formal requests for information. Dunleavy Trust is fairly high profile. I would have expected some headed paper to have arrived before your visit. Why the cloak and dagger?'

'I came across her by accident. I'm working this in my own time.'

He clicked his tongue.

'You be careful, my young friend. If I were you, I'd tell your people about her and get them involved. That's my tuppenceworth, anyway.'

'Look, if it gets too hairy, I'll ask for assistance. As of the moment, I'm just a concerned citizen helping out an old friend. I feel bad about having left her and never bothering to get in contact . . . see how she was doing.'

'You were here for eight weeks a decade ago. You stay in touch with all the kids you work with?'

'No.'

He stood up and shook my hand. 'You know where

the copier is. If there's anything else we can do, let me know. If I were you, though, I'd ring social services, call it in, and forget about her. You're only digging a hole for yourself.'

'I'll keep that in mind.'

There was an open-air market on the street where Sylvie and her father lived. Stalls with flowers, second-hand clothes, sweets and power-tools lined each side of the road, the air thick with the cries of the owners. I wandered through the hustle and noise for some time, pondering how I would handle the girl this time. I did not want her to bolt again.

There was no intercom or buzzer system on the door of their building, just a row of weathered-looking doorbells, none of which had any identifying features. I pressed them all and then stood back, lighting a cigarette as I waited. After five minutes I rang again, holding several bells down for a good thirty seconds. This time I heard heavy footsteps coming downstairs, and the door was flung open by a heavy-set woman in a summer dress that, I noted with deep regret, left little to the imagination.

'Who're you?' she said with vehemence.

'I'm looking for the Lambes.'

'Top floor,' she said, turning her acned back and stumping back up the stairs.

The building smelt of stale tobacco, cooking fat and unwashed humanity. The stairs were carpeted, but the covering was, in many places, so threadbare I could see the wooden boards beneath. The stairs ran up to a third floor, which was in the attic. There was only one door on

147

that level, painted a cracked blue. I banged on it sharply.

Sylvie answered my knocks. She was dressed in a sloppy T-shirt and blue leggings, her hair tousled from sleep and her make-up still on, smudged and messed from the night before. In her arms she held a child of about nine months, also dark-haired, looking at me with huge liquid eyes and sucking a pink soother. The familial resemblance was unmistakable.

'Shane . . .' There was fear in her voice.

'Hey, Sylvie,' I said. 'Can I come in?'

She clutched the infant to her. The child sucked furiously on the soother and watched me intently. 'No, I don't want to see you.'

I nodded and looked about me at the decrepit condition of the landing. *Easy*, I thought. *She's still uncertain of you.* 'It was wrong of me to come on so strong, before, Sylvie. I can understand you being nervous. I just . . . I only wanted to help. I guess I freaked you out a little.'

'You did.'

She cuddled the baby, rubbing her cheek on its thick black hair.

'That's a beautiful child, Sylvie.'

'I know.'

'A girl?'

'Gloria.'

'That's a good name. It's a word of praise, of celebration.'

'I named her after Gloria Gaynor.'

I smiled at the appropriateness.

'*I Will Survive.*'

'Yes.'

'She's your daughter.'

'Yes.'

Although I had known the answer would be affirmative, I suddenly wanted to cry. It came on me in a rush, and I had to grit my teeth and force it right back down. I have a mental exercise I use when something like that happens. I see the feeling as a sheet of paper – the colour differs depending on the feeling: anger is red, pain is black, fear is white, sadness is blue. In my head, I crumple the paper up into a tiny ball and toss it into a bin, one of those pedal ones, where the lid opens and closes. Once that lid snaps closed, the feeling is gone. I can take it out and deal with it later, but for that moment it does not exist. I did the exercise, and if the deep sadness that washed over me showed in my face, Sylvie seemed unaware of it. *For the love of God*, I thought, *she's just a baby herself.*

'Can I come in, please? I'm not going to lose the head today. You showed me that wouldn't work.'

She nodded and stepped back into the flat.

The interior was worn and ragged but very clean and tidy. The dwelling seemed primarily to be made up of a large living room, with four doors leading off it to the left: a small kitchen, two bedrooms and a tiny bathroom. A selection of newish toys for Gloria was on the rug in front of a tattered beige couch. I sat down. A portable television, with the sound muted, was playing a daytime soap.

'What do you want, Shane?' Sylvie sat opposite me on an armchair that belonged to a different suite of furniture to the couch. There was another armchair in the other corner of the room, similarly orphaned.

'To see how you are, to apologize, and to try and persuade you to let me help you. Why didn't you tell me about Gloria, Sylvie?'

'I didn't think I'd ever see you again. What difference would it have made?'

'Is the father still around? Is he helping out?'

She stared at me, a wistful expression on her face. For a moment I was puzzled, then reality dawned.

'Who's the father, Sylvie?'

She laughed cynically and placed the tot onto the floor among the toys. The baby gurgled contentedly and crawled over to a large plastic telephone and picked up the orange receiver. 'Probably my dad, but there were a couple of johns who wouldn't use rubbers.'

'Sylvie, tell me that you're using protection! Jesus, girl, you know better than that. You could catch anything!'

'You try and tell an eighteen-stone drunk that you want him to use a condom when he's already on top of you. Just see how you get on.'

I shook my head. This was going from bad to worse.

'Have you been checked out for sexually transmitted infections?'

'What do you think?'

'Will you let me organize *that* at the very least?'

'Maybe. We'll see.'

'Do you have everything you need? Nappies, wipes, formula, baby food, clothes for her . . .'

'Yeah. We're fine that way.'

'Has the public health nurse been out?'

'Once.'

'What did you tell her?'

'That I got drunk at a friend's house and one of the boys there must have had sex with me when I was out of it. She believed me. Why wouldn't she?'

'There haven't been any social workers out?'

'I'm almost fourteen. I have three friends on this road who are around my age and have babies. It's not *that* weird. Now, you can go ahead and call the social workers –'cause I know that's what you're thinkin' – and they can come out if they want. I have me story straight and nobody can prove otherwise.'

'There's DNA tests now, Sylvie. If she's your dad's . . .'

'And such things cost a lot of money. Do you think they'll bother with stuff like that for me? They've got bigger fish to fry.'

She was right, and I knew it. I had no proof of abuse of any kind, and Sylvie's father had been checked out by social services before she had been placed with him. It would be a struggle to even get a social worker to visit. The case would go on the books and could sit there for a year before it got any attention.

'Can I ask you a question then?'

'I might not answer it.'

'Fair enough, but I'm gonna ask anyway. You don't like being a hooker?'

'Of course I don't.'

'You know that what your dad is doing to you is not right.'

'Yeah.'

'You'd prefer not to bring your little girl up around a man like him?'

'Well . . . yeah.'

'So why won't you come with me? Why won't you let me help you?'

'Fuck sake, Shane. Loads of reasons. Too many to tell you.'

'Try me. Give me one good reason.'

'They'll take Gloria away from me.'

'Not necessarily. There are plenty of places where you could get help and support and still have her.'

'You can't guarantee they'd let me keep her. Can you tell me one hundred per cent for certain, no matter what, they they wouldn't take her from me?'

I looked at my hands and struggled with what she'd just said.

'Nothing is ever one hundred per cent, Sylvie.'

'I knew it. There'd be no problem finding a foster home for a little baby; any family would be glad to have her. It'd be just like having a baby all of their own, except the hard part's done. I *know* they'd take her from me.'

'It's not as simple as that, hon. You'd have to show them that you can manage her and that you're a competent mother. Once you'd done that, they'd surely leave her with you. Nobody *wants* to take children away from their parents.'

'Don't they? That's not how it feels to me. And tell me this. Suppose my da *is* Gloria's da too. Does he have rights to her then? Could he come in eight years' time, if she was in care someplace, and take her, like he took me? I mean, maybe his rights are double, seein' as he's her da *and* her granda.'

'Sylvie, I promise you that is not the case.'

'Are you sure? Because I find it hard to believe what

you people say to me. I was told that I'd be safe, that everythin' would be great, that my da loved me and wanted to mind me. And guess what? He *doesn't* love me, and he never minded me at all. How can I believe anythin' you say?'

'Nobody lied to you, Sylvie. They made a mistake, but it wasn't a lie.'

She fell silent, anger causing her cheeks to flush red beneath the caked make-up.

'I was worried that there'd be somethin' wrong with her,' she said after a while. 'I heard somewhere that if a dad and a daughter do it, that stuff don't work right.'

I nodded. 'Yeah, sometimes that can happen. But she seems to be perfect, doesn't she?'

'She is. In every way.'

'You know she's his daughter, don't you?'

'Look at her. I look like him, and all I can see in her is me. Them other fellas, the tricks, I remember them fairly well, and there's not a bit of either of them in her. It don't matter, though, who she came from. She's mine. That's all I care about.'

'Who watches her when you're working?'

'There's a woman downstairs. I give her a few quid. Gloria's very good at night though. She sleeps right through. Never wakes.'

'What does your father make of her?'

'Who knows? He never passes any comment on her. He beat the shit out of me when I told him I was pregnant. He probably hoped I'd lose her, but I didn't.'

'And how are you handling being a mum? You're so young.'

She looked at her little daughter, burbling happily into the toy phone, and her eyes suddenly filled up. She fought back the tears, clearing her throat and wiping them away with her hand. 'She's so gorgeous. I want her to have all the things I didn't. I want her to know she's loved every minute of every day she's alive. I work extra hard so that I can keep a little back to buy her what she needs – toys that'll help her learn so that she'll be real smart, and nice clothes, and the best food, so that she'll grow up big and strong. He knows I do it, but he don't care so long as he gets the amount he asks for. She's the best thing that has ever happened to me. I never found lookin' after her hard. I like it.'

I reached over and took her hand.

'I'm glad, Sylvie. I'm glad she makes you happy. You deserve a little happiness. But you need support, too. It's nothing to be ashamed of. Nobody can do it all on their own; even adults need help with small babies. Mother-and-toddler groups, that kind of thing.'

'No. I don't *need* any help. I bought books, and I read them all – it was hard, but I read 'em. I listened real good in the hospital when they showed me how to change her nappies and bath her and stuff. I'm a good mother. She looks happy, don't she?'

'She looks very happy and healthy, sweetheart.'

'So you see? Everything's good.'

'But what about *you*? I'm worried about you, Sylvie. You're thirteen years old. You should be in school. The biggest problem in your life should be having too much homework. You should be spending your money on CDs

154

and clothes and going to teenage discos at the weekend. Do you even go to school?'

She hung her head and the child she really was subverted the young woman she played. 'How can I go? I would if I could, I swear.'

'Your father sexually and physically abuses you. As a prostitute, you are being molested nightly. I can't even begin to imagine what that must be doing to you inside. There are people you can talk to, anonymously, who won't put any pressure on you to go into care.'

She shook her head vigorously. 'No, no, no! I'm sortin' it out in my own way. I want you to go now, please. Thanks for callin' and all, but I need to feed my baby.'

I stood up. 'I'll come and see you again. Maybe we could go for a coffee some afternoon? You could bring Gloria.'

'I usually don't go out durin' the day except to go shoppin'. Dad doesn't like it.'

The conversation was over. She had shut down to me. I left them.

There was a pub across the road from the house with tables outside on the pavement, so customers could enjoy the beautiful weather. I ordered a soda water and sat, watching the passers-by. From my back pocket I took a photograph. It had come from her file, and was taken the day Sylvie had left the residential unit. In it she stood at the gate, ready to get into the taxi that would take her to her new life, a skinny nine-year-old, not all that different from the person she was now, in fact. A little shorter and a lot happier, a child full of hope about to be dashed to smithereens. She was hand-in-hand with her father.

I examined the details of the man closely. He looked slightly shorter than me, and skinny. There was grey in his hair, which was as dark as his daughter's except for the slight peppering. He was wearing a woollen pullover and ill-fitting jeans. I looked at his face. He was smiling into the lens, and I could not discern a trace of his intent. I looked at the photo for a long time, until I was certain I would know him if I saw him, and then put it away.

My soda water was gone, so I ordered coffee and a ham sandwich, and asked the waitress if they had the paper. The morning drifted into early afternoon, and slowly became evening. The bar began to fill with the after-work crowd. My nerves jangled with caffeine and nicotine, but still I sat. At five twenty-five he came up the street, round-shouldered and actually shorter than I had reckoned. He also looked greyer than in the picture, and even thinner. His jeans flapped around his legs, and his shirt billowed about him. He wore sandals with no socks, and the butt of a roll-up hung from the corner of his mouth. He walked with the nervous gait of someone who is always on his guard. I watched as he put a key in the lock of the front door, looked about him one last time, and went in. I stood slowly and stretched, paid for my last drink and walked slowly to where I had parked my car. It had a ticket – the money I'd put in the meter had long since run out.

I'll know you, you little bastard, I thought as I turned for home. *Next time, I'll know you.*

9

At eight o'clock the following morning I left the gym, freshly showered and resplendent with the cheap after-shave they kept in the dressing rooms. I opened the boot of the Austin and chucked my gear bag inside, then sat in and pulled out of the parking lot into the steadily growing stream of traffic. After picking up a copy of the *Irish Independent* and the latest *Empire*, I went to a little café not too far from the office, and ordered scrambled eggs, wholegrain toast and a pot of black coffee. It was already a hot day outside, and the morning seemed pregnant with possibility. Despite the events of the previous day, I was in a good mood.

Pouring my third cup, I spotted him, seated three tables ahead of me and trying to hide behind a rumpled *Irish Sun*. I had to look a couple of times to be certain, but he was doing a bad job of being inconspicuous. I thought about going over, but then decided against it and turned back to the Leader page of my newspaper. As soon as I did so, he peered out from behind the tabloid at me again, then surreptitiously ducked undercover. He might as well have cut a hole in it to peep through; he would only have been moderately more obvious.

He was the young man who had watched me leave Mina's workshop the day I had discussed sex, the universe and everything with Ellen. That afternoon he was wearing a garish, knitted jumper. This particular morning he sported a psychedelic, tie-dyed T-shirt, which was so bright it made my fillings hurt. Why he'd followed me into the café, I had no idea. He seemed to want to observe me, and I guessed that there was something he wanted to ask. He'd get to it in his own time.

Half an hour later I pushed my chair back and strolled past him to the counter. I gave him a nod as I went by, but he almost put the paper over his head to avoid being seen. I sat in the car for several minutes, waiting for him to leave the café. He rushed out, spotted me watching him and immediately stopped, turning away and putting his hands behind his back and gazing at the window of the newsagents beside him. I shook my head in puzzlement and drove the short distance to work. As I parked across the road from Dunleavy House, I saw the lad pulling up several spaces behind on a Honda 50 moped. He had a very stylish, sporty helmet, which covered his face, but his explosively coloured top made him instantly recognizable.

I had some administration to catch up on, so I did not linger. If my new friend wanted to talk to me, he knew where I was.

I spent an hour writing and filing reports, then went up to the small library that occupied the loft of the building. I wanted to research an idea I had been considering for the Byrnes. The old building had a well-insulated roof, so the attic-space was always cool. The room contained a couple of saggy but comfortable armchairs, and was lined with bookshelves that contained classics in the fields of psychology and sociology, along with a mixture of other texts, everything from fairy-tales to the collected works of Enid Blyton, medical books to huge tomes on various aspects of the law. It was a strange, yet somehow wholly appropriate, selection. I had spent quite a bit of time there since beginning work with the Trust. There was rarely anyone else among the dust and paper, so I found that I could lose myself in the pages.

Larry had been weighing on my mind. We'd tried a range of methods, none of which had really made any impact on the boy. Francey had begun to come round, partly through the realization that we were as stubborn as her, and partly because of concern for her brother. But Larry had retreated into himself and a complex fantasy about what his life had been. Well, if it was fantasy he wanted, then fantasy he would get.

Children love stories. I have yet to meet a child, even one with a profound intellectual disability, who will not repond positively to being read or told a story, once the tale has been chosen carefully and is at the right level. I thought that perhaps we could begin to do some story-telling work with Larry. I wanted to use traditional fairy-tales. I thought that, with all that he had experienced, they might well be the most resonant for him.

Fairy-tales have a long, intricate history. There are cave drawings dating back to the Neolithic period that depict the story of *Hansel and Gretel*. There are versions of *Cinderella* in every culture, even those that could not possibly have been in contact with one another. Anthropologists who were the first white people to encounter tribes in the African Basin have discovered versions of *Snow White*.

These folk-tales seem to exist independently of us, and appear to be completely universal.

They are also extremely dark. If you stop for a moment and think about the content of all the popular fairy-tales, you'll find that they are actually pretty scary. Take two I've already mentioned: *Hansel and Gretel* deals with children being abandoned, left to die in a great forest, and being captured by a cannibalistic child killer; *Cinderella* is about a little girl being singled out from her siblings by a wicked stepmother to be neglected and abused, made to sleep in the cellar among the ashes of the fire for warmth. Almost all these stories deal with some kind of abuse directed at a child, feature monsters or witches, and involve some form of death or mutilation.

Over the past twenty years, there has been a move among publishers, egged on by the politically correct brigade, to sanitize the traditional tales. So we have *The Three Little Pigs* realizing that the wolf is really angry because he is homeless, and, rather than scalding him to death and eating him in a stew, the porcine trio build him a nice house and make friends with him. In the original telling of *Snow White*, the wicked Queen is captured and brought to the wedding of her estranged stepdaughter, where, as a form of post-reception entertainment, the prisoner is placed in a pair of metal shoes, which are then heated in the fire until they are red-hot, and is made to dance until she drops dead from pain and exhaustion. This ending, funnily enough, has been excised from the modern versions of the story.

But psychologists and child protection experts have long seen the value of the older, more sinister fables. As

I sat in the cramped library, under the slanted eav the roof, I leafed through a book by the great, th disgraced, psychologist Bruno Bettelheim. Bettelheim led a fairly dark life himself, emerging from the death camps of the Second World War as the voice of the disenfranchised. Freud, fleeing the Holocaust, had died in exile in 1939, and the world craved a successor. If there was ever a time when humanity needed someone to make sense of all the madness, it was then. Bettelheim stepped forward, just liberated from Dachau, an emaciated, hollow-eyed creature with a quiet tone and deep charisma, claiming to have been a student of Freud's. He became an international celebrity, and was invited to run a residential unit attached to the University of Chicago, 'the orthogenic school'. He wrote books on various aspects of childcare and social-care, most of which were bestsellers.

Then, without warning, Bettelheim committed suicide in 1990, on the anniversary of the day the Nazis invaded his native Austria. It emerged that an exposé of his life was about to be published, declaring that he had lied about his qualifications (his Ph.D. was in philosophy, rather than psychology; he had never even met Freud, let alone studied under him) and that there had been instances of physical abuse in some of the childcare settings he had run. There also seemed to be a great deal of resentment about the fact that he had had the audacity to kill himself. This was seen as a huge betrayal. People like Bettelheim didn't take a load of pills, tie plastic bags over their heads and then hang themselves. They were supposed to be above that kind of carry-on!

As a result of this revisionism, Bettelheim was all but

written off from the record of child psychology. He is rarely taught now on social-care courses, and a search of the Internet will produce little information on him, short of the report he did for the newly formed United Nations on the psychological impact of the concentration camps on prisoners and SS officers alike. However, I must admit to a lasting affection (and yes, a certain amount of pity) for Bruno Bettelheim, or Dr B, as he came to be called by his posthumous biographers. It seems that he saw the horrors of the war as an opportunity to reinvent himself, to rebuild a shattered life, to rise phoenix-like from the ashes of a charred Europe. Isn't that a wonderful symbol for what social care is really all about: glorious rebirth?

The Uses of Enchantment is Bettelheim's book on story-telling as a therapeutic tool. I read it when I was a student and I remember being struck by the concept that things as seemingly innocuous as stories could be used to heal children of deep emotional wounds. According to the book, fairy-tales contain subconscious symbols, arche-typal images that we all respond to without even knowing it. They deal with issues of kinship, morality, inner strength, betrayal, loss, the predatory nature of real, human monsters. When some shaman, sitting with his people around a fire in a cave in the mountains, first channelled these folk-tales from the ether, they were not meant for children. They were told as a way of making sense of what lurked in the shadows. They told of how people – even small, seemingly helpless people, like chil-dren – can overcome what appear to be insurmountable odds and come out the other side, scarred and shaken, but whole nonetheless. They were a gentle, sometimes beautiful, always fun way of discussing what is frightening and threatening. Because in the dark years of the infancy of our species, there really were wolves hiding in the thickets, and, if you strayed from the path, they were all too ready to pounce.

This world has changed considerably since then. The forests that tend to be the setting for fairy-tales are all but gone. They have been replaced by terrain of a different kind, dangerous in a less obvious way. But the stories continue to remind us of the witch in her cottage, of sweets and cake, of the demonic Rumpelstiltskin, with his twisted desire to have a child, of the troll that hides beneath the bridge, waiting for the unwary to cross . . . and these reminders make us uncomfortable. So we change the stories, contriving to make them more palatable for our arrogant, modern sensibilities. Yet the shadow in the fairy-tale abides. You can dress up the witch or the wolf any way you wish, but their essence remains. They are predators.

I closed the book and, creakily getting to my feet, took the couple of steps to the shelf of children's books. I ran my finger along the titles: Lewis Carroll; Roald Dahl . . . there it was! A long spine, bound in brown leather, with the entwined letters B and G. The Brothers Grimm. I opened it, feeling a slightly childish thrill. Here there were dragons and much, much more.

It was a beautiful book. Each page of text was accompanied opposite by a beautiful plate, painted by the artist Fritz Kedel, depicting a scene from the story. This edition contained a scholarly introduction to the tales, and was published in 1931. But the stories were all here, in their initial, untainted form. I turned to the account of Hansel and Gretel, with which I intended to begin the sessions with Larry. The first plate showed the children, seated on the ground by a dying fire, their arms around each other, alone in the forest. The painter had rendered their faces in loving detail, and their fear, loneliness and sadness were very clear. In the corner of the picture, so small you would barely see it unless you looked very closely, was the silhouette of a wolf's head, its great tongue lolling out. About, all was darkness, the trees looming threateningly around the children. The picture might as well have depicted Larry and Francey. It summed up perfectly what they were like when I had first met them. I read a couple of lines:

Hard by a great forest dwelt a poor wood-cutter with his wife and his two children. The boy was called Hansel and the girl Gretel. He had little to bite and to break, and once, when great scarcity fell on the land, he could no longer procure daily bread . . .

The language was a bit archaic, but then, so was Larry and Francey's. I didn't think it would be a problem. I closed the book and looked at my watch. I had been in the library for two hours, and it was lunchtime.

I grabbed my jacket from the back of the chair in my office, called to Jerome, who was the only other staff-member in that day, that I was heading out, and went into the bright sunlight. There was a sandwich stand two roads over, and I made for it, whistling as I walked, my head now on frivolous things. Somebody touched me on the shoulder and I turned, almost falling over in surprise. I was staring into a blank, reflective visage, a bit like Darth Vader's mask. I stumbled back a step, raising a hand to ward off the spectre, when realization dawned.

'You have to tell me what you wants with Mina!' it said.

My shadow from the morning had decided to make his move. I almost laughed. He was still wearing the helmet, which had one of those hi-tech, mirrored visors, so I could not see his face. Under it was the imaginatively coloured T-shirt, which fought valiantly to contain a pot-belly.

'Hey . . .' I said, regaining my composure, 'we haven't been introduced yet.'

'You been axin' about my Mina, and I wants to know what you has to do with her! You have to tell me now!'

I stared dumbly, unsure how to proceed.

'Why don't you take the helmet off and tell me your name?'

'Oh, no!' The figure's voice was muffled under the protective headgear. 'You don't know what I look like, and you won't find out neither!'

'You were watching me at the workshop the last time I was there. You were in the café this morning, and you followed me here on a Honda 50. You've got curly light-brown hair.'

'Oh.'

'Now, take off the helmet. You must be sweating in there. Have you had it on all morning?'

The head nodded, a bit cowed, having learned that all the subterfuge had come to nothing. I felt a little guilty. I probably should have played along a bit more.

'Why did you keep it on even when I was inside?'

'My mammy says that it'll get robbed if I leave it down.'

The chubby face was rolling with sweat when the helmet finally came off, the curls plastered to his scalp. I guessed he was in his late teens, maybe as old as twenty, but no more than that.

'What's your name?'

'I'm Jacob Benedict and I am very pleased to meet you.' His hand was thrust out to me, the introduction rattled off as if learned by rote, which it probably was.

I shook the proffered hand, smiling at him.

'Well, Jacob Benedict, I'm very pleased to meet you, too. Any friend of Mina's is a friend of mine.'

'You can call me Jake, if you like. Are you Mina's friend?'

'Yes, I am. I'm Shane.'

'Like the western.'

'You know the western?'

'Yeah! Alan Ladd and Jack Palance! My daddy says that Shane dies at the end, but I don't think so. You don't see him die. I think he gets better.'

'You know, that's always what I thought, too. It's a better ending, isn't it?'

He nodded vigorously.

'I'm hungry,' he said, biting his lower lip, nervously. 'I've been out since early and I didn't have enough money for anything except a cup of tea.'

'I was just off to get a sandwich. Want one?'

'I ain't got no money.'

'I'll get you this one. Why don't we leave that helmet in my office. It'll be safe, I promise.'

He looked uncertain.

'My mammy'd kill me if it got stoled.'

'I tell you what. We'll get Mrs Munro to watch it. She's kind of scary, but she's nice really, and when you meet her, you'll see that there isn't anyone who'll steal your helmet if she's watching it.'

Mrs Munro was the stern secretary of the Trust. She was actually, once you got to know her, a gentle and kind woman, but it took some time and no little effort to see that.

'It's a pretty cool helmet,' I commented as we walked back.

'Yeah! It makes you go faster.'

'Does it?'

'Daddy says so.'

'Well, it must be true then.'

Mrs Munro took Jacob's helmet gravely, and told him that she would guard it with her life. He beamed from ear to ear, and left to get his sandwich with a much lighter step.

'Ain't *nobody* goin' to get it off of her!'

'Told you.'

Chatting about nothing in particular, we walked to the sandwich stand.

'What would you like, Jake?'

'I would like a ham sandwich and a Coke and a packet of crisps and a Mars Bar.'

'Hungry, huh?'

'Yeah,' he nodded, wide-eyed, carefully watching his sandwich being constructed.

I got tuna salad on brown and an iced tea for myself,

and we made our way back to the duck pond and sat on a bench in the midday sun.

'So why've you been following me?'

He couldn't answer me for a few minutes. He had shovelled one half of the sandwich right into his mouth, along with a fistful of crisps.

'Hey, slow down, there. You'll give yourself a pain.'

'You was axin' about my Mina,' he finally managed. 'Then she stopped comin' into work. Why she stop? What've you done with her?'

'I haven't done anything with her, Jake. Her mother and father decided they wanted to keep her at home for a bit. I'm afraid I can't tell you why. It's a family thing. Private, y'know?'

He popped the Coke can and gulped most of the contents in great slurps, then belched resonantly.

'Me 'n' Mina is goin' steady.'

I looked at the young man beside me. I never would have put the two of them together. Mina, despite her disability, was prim, proper and well spoken. Jacob was scruffy, over-weight, ill-mannered and not too articulate. Yet there was also a sweetness and decency about him that was undeniable. He and Mina were on slightly different levels, but then, aren't we all? And he was obviously crazy about her. He had taken it upon himself to find out where I lived and worked and, despite discomfort, had stuck with me until hunger had smoked him out. It was quite impressive, really.

'How long have you been going steady, Jake?'

'Long time.'

'Since, say, before last Christmas?'

He stopped chewing for a moment and screwed up his

eyes, concentrating. Time can be a particularly difficult concept for people with certain intellectual disabilities.

'Last Christmas I got my bike and my helmet,' he muttered. 'And I showed it to Mina when we went back to work after the holidays! So yeah, she was my girlfriend then.'

'What makes her your girlfriend?'

'What do you mean?'

'Well, what's different about you and Mina from, say, you and one of the other girls you work with who isn't your girlfriend?'

'I loves Mina and she loves me.'

'Has she told you that she loves you?'

'Oh yeah. Oh yeah, she tells me every day when we're at work.'

'That's nice. Anything else different?'

'We kisses sometimes,' he whispered. 'When no one's watchin' us.'

I nodded.

'Do the staff know? Ellen and them?'

'No. We're not let be boyfriend and girlfriend at work. They get mad if they catches you. They don't mind so much at the club. I mean, we only hold hands there. You shouldn't kiss and stuff when people are watchin' you. It's rude.'

'That's true. And what do your mum and dad think of you having a girlfriend?'

'My mammy and daddy don't mind. Mina's won't let her, though.'

'She told you that?'

He nodded, peeling the paper off the Mars Bar and nibbling at the chocolate outer layer. It was strange after watching the decimation of the rest of the food to see him approach the confection so delicately.

'And why won't they let her?'

'I dunno,' he shrugged. The Mars had most of the chocolate off it by now, the nougat and caramel a two-tone block, with a small section at the end still chocolate-coated so he could hold it. He started to lick the caramel.

'What does Mina think?'

'She says that' – he bunched up his face again, straining to recall the memory – 'she says that her parents think she is a child, even though she is an adult, and they want to keep her tied to her mother's apron strings for as long as possible.'

'I see.' I crumpled my sandwich wrapper and tossed it into the bin opposite us. I took out a cigarette and was about to light it.

'I don't like smoking,' Jacob said, his eyes still on the duck pond. 'It smells nasty and makes my eyes sting and . . . and it makes me cough.'

I put the cigarette back in the packet, not even bothering to suppress a smile. There were depths to Jacob.

'Does Mina tell you why she sometimes runs away?' I ventured, flicking open and closed the lid of my Zippo for want of anything else to do with my hands.

Jacob looked at me from the corner of his eye.

'She tells me everything,' he said matter-of-factly, and began to bite small, even pieces off the remaining nougat.

'Would you like to tell me about that?'

'No.'

'I want to help her, Jake. She's not happy now, and it's all mixed up with her running away.'

'She told me not to tell no one.'

'You know, there are good secrets and bad secrets.'

'We talked all about secrets when I was at school,' he said, bristling. 'I know all about that. I'm not a kid! "Yes feelings" and "No feelings"! What's that got to do with all this stuff?'

'I'm sorry, Jacob. I didn't mean to offend you.'

'You people always think I'm stupid. I'm not, you know. I'm a little bit slow, sometimes, but I'm not thick in my head. I understand a lot of things.'

'I'm really sorry. I know you're not stupid, Jacob. I can see that. I don't want to hurt your feelings.'

He sniffed and stuck the last bit of chocolate into his mouth. 'Okay then. We'll say no more about it.'

'Thank you.'

'You're welcome.'

We sat quietly for a few minutes. I wanted to broach Mina's running away again, but didn't know how to without upsetting Jacob. He had a finely tuned sense of dignity, honed over years of being patronized and ridiculed by a society that has little patience and tolerance for people who are different.

'Are you really Mina's friend?' he asked when he'd swallowed his mouthful.

'Yes. I really am. I want to make things right for her, if I can.'

'How do you know her? I've never seen you at the club or anything.'

'That's a bit hard to explain.'

'Are you a social worker?'

'No. But I suppose I'm a little bit like one.'

'How can you help?'

'I don't know, because I still don't really know what the problem is.'

'We want to be able to be together.'

He turned around, and looked me right in the eye. At that moment, all differences were stripped away. We were two men talking, equal to equal.

'I understand,' I said. 'And I will talk to Mina's parents about you and see if I can't maybe get them to reconsider. But how does that have anything to do with Mina running away?'

'She runs away because she is upset in herself.'

'Go on.'

'She wants to be like everyone else. It's hard for Mina, harder than for me, 'cause, see, she looks differenter than other peoples.'

'I can imagine.'

'She runs away and goes to places where they don't know her, and she 'tends to herself that she doesn't look retarded. She knows she still does, but peoples don't seem to notice. She says they treat her as if she's just like any other girl. She says it's great.'

I gathered that Mina had not shared the full extent of her activities with Jacob, and decided not to enlighten him. It would only cause him pain.

'I'm not sure that it's as great as she's letting on, Jake.'

He shrugged. 'I'm just tellin' you what she says. Why would she lie?'

'I don't think she's lying, really. It's just that, sometimes, when you want something to be true badly enough, you actually start to think that it is.'

He stared at the ducks on the water, chewing his lower lip as he thought that over.

'I ain't never goin' to be like everyone else. I know that. I used to want to be, but since I started to get big, I ain't so sure I want to be no more. In the workshop and in the club, peoples is nice. Out in the world, they's mean most of the time, far as I can see. But Mina, she don't see that. She still wishes she was the same as everyone else.'

I said nothing as he made this remarkable statement. What was there *to* say?

'I told her that I wouldn't like her to be normal,' he said after a while.

'Why not?' I asked, knowing the answer before he said it.

''Cause if she was normal,' he said, his voice catching with emotion, 'she wouldn't love me, would she?'

That night I put my mandocello, tenor banjo and harmonicas into their respective cases and got a taxi to The Minstrel Boy. I arrived at ten thirty, and there was already a good selection of musicians in place, covering a gamut of instrumental families: several fiddles, a couple of accordions, some guitars, a man with a box full of percussion instruments and a guy with a bag of tin whistles in different keys. Ben was seated in the corner, his old Spanish guitar across his knees and a pint of ale on the table before him. A twelve-bar blues improv was in full swing, and I put my gear down with the empty cases by the door, went to the bar and ordered a pint of stout. It is part of the etiquette of sessions that you wait to be invited to join in, so I watched my drink settle and listened to the group play. When they finished, Ben waved me over, and introduced me. A space was cleared and I tuned up and got comfortable. A set of reels followed, led by the whistle player. Ben has a nice, percussive finger-style, and he drove the other guitars forward. I fell in on the banjo, playing a kind of rag-time rhythm. The musicians had a mix of styles and it made for an interesting sound.

The night drifted on, and I thoroughly enjoyed myself. It had been a while since I'd played with other people, but I found the fluidity returning to my fingers. Songs and tunes were all greeted with applause and whoops of encouragement from the people in the bar.

After an hour or so, Ben called for hush, and asked me to sing. I nodded assent, and picked up the mandocello. A mandocello is a member of the mandolin family. It has eight strings, a large, tear-shaped body and a neck similar to that of a guitar. Its tone is much deeper than a bou-zouki, to which it is closely related. My mandocello is built along the design of the early English lute, with a diamond-shaped sound-hole and a tapered head. I like it because it has a nice kick to it on faster songs and tunes, but it can be a really melodic, delicate instrument for slower, more intricate, emotive pieces.

I put the appropriate harmonica into its harness, adjusted my capo and told the group that I'd be playing in the key of F.

I'd been thinking, after meeting with Jacob, about the whole idea of love, and how tenuous it can be. I'd also been pondering, from my work on stories that morning, the concept of archetypes. The song that came to me then, as the shadows in the old pub grew longer, and the night reached that point where magic seems to hang in the air, combined both those ideas. It dates back to the time of the Famine in Ireland, and tells the story of a man who has married for money, and accidentally comes across a girl that he once loved, but abandoned because she had no prospects. The melody is painfully beautiful, and once I had plucked the first few chords on the strings and then played the introduction on the harmonica, the others fell in like they'd been playing it all their lives.

> *As I roved out on a bright May morning*
> *To view the meadows and flowers gay,*
> *Whom should I spy but my own true lover*
> *As she sat under yon willow tree.*
>
> *I took off my hat and I did salute her –*
> *I did salute her most courageously.*
> *But she turned around and the tears fell from her*
> *Crying: 'False young man, you have deluded me.'*

There are musicians who believe that some songs and tunes are haunted; that the spirit, not only of the composer, but also of the thousands of musicians who have played them and kept them alive and put their stamp and individual mark on them down through the centuries, enters the room and the hearts of the players when they are performed. This was one of those songs, and everyone in the bar that night felt it. A hush fell as the lyric, written more than a century ago, told the story of the sorrowful meeting of these two lost lovers.

And at nights when I go to my bed of slumber
The thoughts of my true love run in my mind.
But when I turn around to embrace my darling
Instead of gold, sure 'tis brass I find.

And I wish the queen would call home her armies
From the West Indies, America and Spain.
And every man to his wedded woman
In the hopes that you and I may meet again . . .

I led the group through the closing salvo, and we finished together. The hush continued for a long moment, then the room erupted with applause.

'Nice one,' Ben mouthed at me, as the percussionist slapped me on the back.

The music was over. Instruments had been put back into their cases and small groups were gathered around the room, chatting over glasses of whiskey. Ben and I sat at the bar, waiting for a taxi.

'That was a good night,' Ben said.

'It was.'

'Will we see you here again?'

'You will.'

'Excellent. Maybe we'll get a few more songs next time.'

'I'll have to dust some off. I'm a bit rusty.'

'I saw no rust tonight.'

'Nice of you to say so.'

I gestured to the barman for another couple of whiskies.

'How're the cases going?'

'I don't want to talk shop tonight, Ben.'

'Fair enough. I just thought that was an interesting choice of song, that's all.'

'You are a shrewd bastard, aren't you?'

'The Walshes getting to you?'

I looked at him in wonder and pushed my money over the bar as the glasses were placed before us.

'Would you believe, I was thinking of the Byrnes and Henrys when I chose it. But yes, it has parallels with the Walsh situation too.'

'Must be one of those catch-all songs.'

'It must be.'

We sampled the whiskey and sat for a while.

'I wish I knew what was going on with the Walshes though. I am utterly stumped.'

'How so?'

'Ben, they truly believe that they are seeing their dead father. They're so fucking convincing, I'm even starting to believe there's something going on. I mean . . . *could* they be seeing something?'

Ben picked up his glass and gestured with his head. We went out into the beer garden to the rear of the pub. It was empty except for the two of us. The night sky was an explosion of stars, the air still dense with heat. Ben sat down on one of the tables, took out his pouch and started to roll a smoke.

'The answer to your question, Shane,' he said, licking the gummed edge of the cigarette paper, 'is that I don't know. And I'm not sure it's important.'

'It's important to them. It's about the most important thing in their lives.'

'Maybe it's not, though. This is a highly unusual case,

and I think maybe you've started to dwell on the stranger aspects of it. Don't obsess on the weird stuff. What the boys need is closure: an end to this unhappiness and the chance to say goodbye once and for all to their father. I believe he was and is bad for them, but he remains their father and they love him. Help them achieve these things, and the other stuff should follow.'

'I don't see how they can ever get closure when . . . when they're being haunted, Ben. Because, to all intents and purposes, that is what is happening. There's no other way of putting it.'

He exhaled smoke out of his nose and spat a bit of loose tobacco out of the corner of his mouth.

'They may be. They just may. You have to keep an open mind about everything in this work. It's not the first time I've come across apparently supernatural elements to cases. What we need to remember is that these are two upset, frightened little boys, and our job is to help them deal with their pain. You should stop trying to prove or disprove the genuineness of the alleged haunting, and start to focus on what is right for the boys. It would be better if they were away from their father. If he was alive, and we were working on this case, I'd be pushing for some kind of separation. Whatever way you look at it, his influence is malevolent. Now, try and think of it like that. Their father is who he is, regardless of whether he is corporeal or not. Effect a separation.'

I knew he was right. I just wished the case wasn't so damned difficult.

10

Jacob Benedict had given me an idea.

The following Saturday I sat at a table outside the pub opposite where Sylvie, Gloria and their father lived. I arrived just as the bar was opening, and took up my post facing their front door. I didn't think that Mr Lambe would have risen yet, so I ordered some coffee, lit a smoke and read the paper, keeping one eye on the street.

At one thirty a dishevelled Joseph Lambe stepped onto the pavement. He was dressed in a loose-fitting vest that bunched up around the waist of his baggy jeans and displayed a scrawny, hairless chest and sinewy arms, and the same sandals he had been wearing when I had seen him before. A hand-rolled cigarette again hung from his lips, and he had on a cheap pair of imitation Ray-Bans. Several days' worth of stubble adorned his face and his hair stuck up at alarming angles from his head. He looked for all the world like a man in the throes of a wretched hangover. I let him get ten metres or so up the street, then followed, falling into the flow of pedestrians but keeping him in my line of sight.

I didn't know exactly where he was going, but I knew his purpose. He was off to get a cure. I'd never met Joe Lambe in person, but I'd met plenty like him. He was feeling sick to his stomach. His head was pounding, his mouth was dry and his hands wouldn't stop shaking. The only thing that was going to make it all go away was the hair of the dog.

Sure enough, ten minutes later he ducked into a small pub off the main thoroughfare. There was no name over the door, just a small, cracked window, an open door and a sign that said *Bar*. Just the kind of place I would have expected him to frequent – anonymous. I hung outside for five minutes, then went in.

I sensed rather than saw him at a low table by the window. I ordered a soda water and leant on the bar, watching him in my peripheral vision. He had a large bottle of cider and a glass of ice in front of him, but that was for a chaser. He was gulping a large whiskey, and when he had drained the last drop from the glass, he carefully poured the cider over the ice and took a long swallow.

I wanted him to take in just enough so that the Delirium Tremens were under control. It was important that he understood and took in every word I would say to him. I lit a cigarette and waited. There was no hurry. He wasn't going anywhere for a while.

'Frankie, gimme another round,' he called to the barman three minutes later.

'Right y'are, Joey.'

When the drinks were lined up, I winked at Frankie, who was a surprisingly well-groomed man in early middle age. 'I'll drop them down for you.'

'Cheers, bud.'

I picked up the cider and whiskey and went over to where the small man was sitting, rolling another cigarette from a pouch of Old Holborn. I set the glasses on the table, and pulled over a stool. He put the finished product in the corner of his mouth and I struck my Zippo and lit it for him.

'Do I know you, friend?' His voice was thin and reedy, not high-pitched, but with a guttural edge that spoke of cruelty.

'No, you don't know me, Joey. We've never met.'

'Well, how can I be of service to you then?'

He was looking at me closely, trying to sum me up. He had come back to his full faculties rapidly, and a wicked intellect showed in his hooded eyes. He was not a man to underestimate.

'I'd like to chat to you about your daughter. Your *eldest* daughter. Sylvie.'

His eyes narrowed, and he picked up the whiskey and sipped it.

'She usually doesn't do appointments. But if the price is right, as they say . . .'

'That's not why I'm here. You see, I know Sylvie from before you reappeared from whichever stone you'd crawled under. I used to work with her when she was in care. Now, it caused me some distress when I saw that, rather than being in the bosom of a loving foster family, which is what was always intended for her, she'd been placed with a sick, twisted fuck of a father, who sexually and physically abused her and put her out on the game.'

He said nothing, eyeing me closely.

'Give me one reason why I shouldn't kick the living shit out of you right now, you slimy little bastard,' I said.

He stubbed out the cigarette. He was tougher than he looked. I wasn't scaring him.

'What are you? Some kind of social worker? Bleeding fucking heart do-gooder?'

'Something like that. But the meter isn't running now, Joey. This is purely personal.'

He laughed, but stopped quickly. His head hadn't completely stopped aching yet.

'You cunts're all the same. You can talk hard, but you're all fucking mouth. You want a half hour with Sylvia, she's down the docks most nights. You want to get your kicks beatin' up on a sick man, well let's go outside and you can take your shot. I've taken hidin's before and you don't frighten me. But if this is all you've got to say, fuck off and let me enjoy my afternoon pints, will you?'

'You don't get off that easy.'

'What are you gettin' at, bud? Make your point, will you?'

'I know where you live. I know where Sylvie works. I know that you have fathered a child by her. I want you to take her off the streets, and I want you to stop raping her and beating her. If I find that you have continued, I will be all over you with social workers and cops so fast you won't even feel the impact. You won't be able to take a piss without being watched. I am giving you this one chance – a chance you don't deserve – to get your act together. Consider what I say very carefully, because I mean every fucking word of it. Do you understand me?'

He looked at me silently for a second.

'She's only a little whore,' he said in disgust, spitting

the words at me. 'What do you care about a little whore?'

Before I knew I'd done it, I knocked the table over and had him by the front of his vest against the wall. Glass crunched on the floor beneath my boots. Cider ran across the floorboards.

'She is a whore because you made her one,' I said through gritted teeth. 'You've worked your poison on her for long enough. Take her off the streets tonight, do you hear me?'

He was staring right into my eyes. Again, I saw no fear, only resentment. He was a little man who had been pushed around all his life. It was probably why he came back for Sylvie in the first place: he wanted someone to push around. Now, here was someone else, bigger and stronger, pushing him around again.

'I hear you,' he said. 'Loud and clear.'

I shook him like a dog shakes a rabbit.

'Then mark me, Joey. Mark what I say.'

I let him go. Frankie was polishing glasses at the bar, whistling *The Wild Colonial Boy*. It seemed that outbursts like this were not uncommon in his establishment. I walked out the door, suddenly realizing that I was shaking and that my eyes were wet.

'Another round, Frankie,' I heard Joseph Lambe call before the door closed. Business as usual.

I stood at Mina's bedroom door. Her parents were outside in the preened garden, drinking lemonade, enjoying the sunshine and listening to classical music on Lyric FM. Mina was still walled up in her boudoir, refusing to see or speak to anyone. I'd had enough of it, and told her so.

'You can't stay in there for ever. I'm not leaving until you see me. I've got a sleeping bag in the car, and I'll go and get it. How would you like to have me out here, singing sea shanties at three o'clock in the morning? I'll do it. Don't say I didn't warn you.'

Implacable silence. There was a smell of roses and pollen from the open window at the end of the landing. Inside, the house was cool and had that odd atmosphere houses have when they are empty. I always felt like a trespasser at the Henrys' anyway, but it was worse when I was on my own. Mina was there, but she seemed out of place too. That was probably a big part of the problem.

'Jacob came to see me,' I said, deciding it was time to pull the ace out of the deck. 'We had a long talk.'

I waited, listening intently for movement behind the door. Nothing for a second, then a key rattled, and it opened. Mina stood in the space, her hair tousled; she was dressed in shorts and a faded T-shirt with Care Bears on it.

'Hey there, stranger,' I said.

'What did Jacob say?'

'He told me he loved you and you loved him, and that the workshop and your parents didn't want you to be together. He said that was why you've been running away. You're unhappy because you're different, and can't do the things "normal" people do, so you go where people don't know you, and try to do all the stuff you aren't allowed to do at home.'

A tear rolled down her cheek. She wiped at it absently.

'Is that about it, Mina? You have to tell me, or I can't do anything to help.'

'Yes,' she said, turning and going back into the room, but leaving the door open, now.

Her room was in an advanced state of disarray. Plates and bowls were strewn here and there, most with bits of partially eaten food encrusted onto them. Clothes, magazines and CD cases lay on the floor. The window was closed, and there was a smell of humanity lingering in the air. Mina sat on the unmade bed and pulled her knees up to her chin.

'I love him. He's a beautiful person. He's not smart or handsome or tough, but he's gentle and decent and he loves me for who I am, not what he wants me to be or thinks I should be.'

'He doesn't know about your . . . um . . . activities in The Sailing Cot.'

A look of panic. 'No! You didn't tell him, did you?'

'No. I didn't want to hurt him. I don't suppose you want to tell me exactly what *did* happen, by any chance, because I'm still a bit confused –'

'No, it doesn't matter, anyway. You can't help. No one can help.'

'Well, thanks for the vote of confidence.'

'They', she gestured with her head at the window, 'can't stand the sight of Jacob. He's below me. And anyway, they don't want me to have a boyfriend. They think I'm still a child.'

'All parents feel that way about their children, Mina. It's part of being a parent. It doesn't mean they don't love you, and it doesn't mean that they can't learn to see things differently. You're still very young. Seventeen is not *exactly* adulthood, you know. Give them a chance. Let me talk to them.'

She shook her head and sighed deeply. A wistful look had come over her, and she didn't seem to be really with me any more.

'We've talked about getting married, some day. We'd have to run away together, and Jacob's very afraid of leaving his parents, but he said he'd go, for me. We'd get a little house, somewhere, and I'd keep a garden, maybe grow some vegetables to sell. Jacob could work in a shop or a factory. He could do that; it wouldn't be too hard. We wouldn't have much money, but we'd have enough.' She looked at me, her eyes soft with sadness. 'Isn't that a lovely dream, Shane?'

'It sounds wonderful. I'd like to come and visit, if you'd have me.'

She laughed with no humour at all.

'It's just a dream, stupid. Go and talk to Mum and Dad. Good luck with it. Maybe then you'll see what I mean.'

Insects droned in the flowers and hedges of the Henrys' garden, and the sound of the ornamental fountain was like liquor over ice. Molly and Dirk sat in front of me, and they were not happy people.

'We are familiar with this Jacob person,' Dirk said. 'We have discussed the issue at length with Mina, and I thought that it had been settled. He is not a suitable person for her to be associating with. Not suitable by any means.'

'He seemed to be a nice guy when I met him.'

'That is neither here nor there,' Molly said.

'Surely it is. I mean, if he's a decent bloke and you know him . . . I just don't see the problem.'

'There are several rather pertinent problems,' Dirk said.

He was dressed in a snazzy polo-shirt and shorts combo with dazzlingly white tennis shoes. His sunglasses probably cost more than my car.

'Enlighten me,' I said, 'because I think that we might just be able to sort out this entire mess.'

'Mina and Jacob are from different . . . different echelons of society,' Dirk said, looking uncomfortable just speaking about Mina's suitor. 'The Benedicts are nice enough people, but they are, well . . . Jacob's father works in a factory, for God's sake!'

'Their home is a tiny little place,' Molly continued. 'Terraced.'

I shook my head in disbelief. 'You are trying to tell me that you won't let Mina have a relationship with this boy whom she obviously adores because he comes from a working-class background? Tell me you're not serious.'

'There is more to it than that,' Dirk said irritably. 'There is the whole issue of the . . . er . . . the physicality.'

'The sex,' I helped him out.

'Yes.'

'Mina is not worldly,' Molly said. 'She does not understand the implications of her actions.'

'You are worried that she may get pregnant.'

'Yes. And there are diseases. It is too complex an issue for someone of her abilities. She's too young.'

'Mina's seventeen, Molly. I'm not suggesting for a second that she and Jacob should be hopping into bed with one another. Most seventeen-year-olds *are*, by the way, but that's another story. They just want to be able to have a relationship out in the open, with your blessing. I don't think that's too much to ask.'

'It's not really your business, Shane, with respect,' Dirk said.

'You asked me to come out here and help you deal with Mina's unhappiness and her running away. I believe that I have found the reason for it. Now, you're telling me that it's none of my business. I'm confused, Dirk.'

'She has not run now in weeks,' Molly said.

'She's been locked in her room! She's embarrassed and miserable. I'd hardly write that up as a victory.'

'I don't see that the running away and her confused feelings for this Jacob boy are connected, anyway,' Dirk said, pouring a glass of lemonade for himself from the ever-present jug.

'I think it's pretty easy to see the link. She believes, correctly, it seems, that she can't have a relationship with him because of her disability. So, she runs away to be off by herself and to try and do what "normal" people do. She may even be looking for Jacob for all I know. It seems she goes to working-class areas. Mina feels stigmatized by her condition. She is craving what everyone else has, and, seeing as she's not allowed to have it here, she looks for it elsewhere.'

'This is purely assumption,' Molly said, getting visibly more annoyed. 'You have not asked Mina.'

'I have. She just told me, for God's sake!'

'We do not have to sit and listen to this rubbish,' she said. 'I would like you to leave, please. We were enjoying a pleasant afternoon before you arrived.'

'You'd better go, Shane,' Dirk said, standing up.

I stood up too. 'I'm sorry if I've upset you, Molly, but please think about what I've said. Mina will run off again, because she doesn't know what else to do. She needs someone to offer her an alternative. It would be lovely if the person to make the offer was you.'

I nodded at Dirk and left. I had said all that I had come to say anyway.

Larry sat, facing the wall as I read to him. He'd been that way for two sessions now, but on this particular evening he glanced over his shoulder at me a couple of times, so I thought that perhaps I was starting to make progress. I had read *Hansel and Gretel* up to where the children had been left in the forest and had followed the trail of pebbles Hansel had dropped, and made their way back home the first time. I read on:

Once more, there was a great scarcity in all parts, and the children heard their mother saying at night to their father, 'Everything is eaten again; we have one half-loaf left, and after that there is an end. The children must go; we will take them farther into the wood, so that they will not find their way out again; there is no other means of saving ourselves!' The man's heart was heavy, and he thought, 'It would be better for thee to share the last mouthful with thy children.' The woman, however, would listen to nothing that he had to say, but scolded and reproached him. As he had yielded the first time, he had to do so a second time.

'He gaveded in again,' Larry said, his face still pressed against the wall.

We were in the sitting room, and it was just after eight o'clock in the evening. The other kids and staff were at various points around the house, so we had the room to ourselves. It was quiet and pleasant in the gentle light as night slowly descended. This special time was Larry's and mine. He had not made any comments on the story before, so I was anxious to capitalize on it.

'Yes. In the story, they seem to be saying, because he gave in the first time, he hadn't much choice but to give in a second time – I'm not so sure about that, though. I think he probably could have said no, if he'd really wanted to.'

'Their mammy din' want them no more. She mus'n'a likened them much, hah?'

'I suppose not. It's hard to say. Sometimes mammys and daddys do bad things, but it doesn't mean they don't love their children. It's really hard for mammys and daddys not to love their children.'

'I bets them kidses . . .'

'Hansel and Gretel.'

'Yeah, them. I bets they was right mad at them there parents.'

'They went back home though, didn't they? Even after they'd been left all alone in the forest.'

'Yeah. They did, too.'

Larry turned around and sat looking at me. I was on a

beanbag, with the big, old book open in my lap. I had pulled another bag over for him, but he had curled up in the corner, on the floor. He scuttled over now, and sat on the beanbag next to me, looking at the picture. It showed the bedroom, with the two parents in bed, talking, and Hansel and Gretel in twin beds at the foot of the larger, marital one, also awake and listening. The dressing table in the room was strewn with make-up bottles, perfume, creams and all the accoutrements of a woman who took scrupulous care of her appearance.

'Lookit all that there stuff,' Larry said, pointing to the cosmetics in the picture.

'All the make-up?'

'Yeah. Maybe if she buyded less of that they could have more t'ate.'

'Maybe.'

'Read some more.'

When the old folks were asleep, Hansel got up and wanted to go out and pick up pebbles, to leave a trail as before, but the woman had locked the door, and Hansel could not get out. Nevertheless he comforted his little sister, and said, 'Do not cry, Gretel, go to sleep quietly. The good God will help us.'

'He means God up in the sky,' Larry said.

'Do you think He lives up in the sky?'

'One of the womens in the last place we was in said that there do be this oul' fella lives in the sky and minds you. Him's called God.'

'And what do you think of that?'

Larry shrugged. 'I dunno. Never did anyt'in' for us. Maybe He don' liken' kids none.'

'I don't think that's true.'

'I reckon she was lyin' anyways.'

'A lot of people believe in God.'

'I don' care abou' dat now. Read some more.'

Early in the morning came the woman, and took the children out of their beds. Their bit of bread was given to them. On the way into the forest, Hansel crumbled his in his pocket and often stood still and threw a morsel on the ground. The woman led the children still deeper into the forest, where they had never in their lives been before. A great fire was made, and the mother said, 'Just sit there, you children, and when you are tired you may sleep a little; we are going into the forest to cut wood and when we are done, we will fetch you away.'

'She's lyin'!' said Larry urgently. 'They's gonna leave them there children in the woods again. You shouldn' do dat to children, so you shouldn'. That's a awful mean, cruel ting to do.'

His voice was thick with anger, and I could feel him trembling. He had cuddled into me, his face pressed into my shoulder.

'Want me to stop?'

'No.'

'Is it making you feel a bit bad?'

He nodded. 'Little bit. But it's only a story.'

'Sometimes stories can make us think of things that might have happened to us. That can be hard.'

He nodded again. 'These be awful mean parents,' he said hoarsely.

They fell asleep, and evening came and went, but no one came to the poor children. They did not awake until it was dark night, and Hansel comforted his little sister, and said, 'Just wait, Gretel, until the moon rises, and then we shall see the crumbs of bread which I have strewn about; they will show us the way home.' When the moon came they set out, but they found no crumbs, for the many thousands of birds which fly about in the woods and fields had picked them all up. Hansel said to Gretel, 'We shall soon find the way,' but they did not find it. They walked the whole night and all the next day, too, from morning till evening, but they did not get out of the forest, and were very hungry, for they had nothing to eat but two or three berries, which grew on the ground.

'They must be fierce hungry,' Larry whispered. 'I know what that do be like. Me 'n' Francey use be rale hungry when they lockded us up. They di'n' use give us hardly anyt'in' t'ate. You git pains 'fore long, in yer belly. There wasn' even any water ou' in that there shed. Sometimes we'd snake out, we'd 'scape, an' we'd catch us birds 'n' such, an' we'd ate them raw. They wasn' nice, but we wasn' hungry no more.'

'How did you know how to catch them, Larry? I don't think I'd be able to catch a bird, no matter how hungry I was.'

'There was this ol' cat what use come into our yard. We could see him t'rough de window of the shed. We use watch him all the time. He'd come up an' sit on the window ledge and we could kinda play wit'im t'rough the glass. He were a right nice cat, so he was. See, he'd catch little birds that'd come down to our yard. We seen how he done it. He'd get down rale low on his belly like, an' snake along on the ground rale slow, and then he'd jump . . . it took us a long time to get it right, but we was so hungry, we keepded on tryin'. There was a field behind our house that no one never went into, and we'd go in dere. Mammy never founded out about it. We'd go back to the shed 'fore she ever knew we was gone.'

'Just like Hansel and Gretel went back.'

He looked at me with big eyes, full now of a pained understanding.

'We di'n' have nowheres else to go.'

After three days, they reached a little house and they saw that it was built of bread and covered with cakes, but that its windows were clear sugar. 'We will set to work on that,' said Hansel, 'and have a good meal. I will eat a bit of the roof, and thou, Gretel, canst eat some of the window, it will taste sweet.' Suddenly the door opened, and a very, very old woman, who supported herself on crutches, came creeping out. Hansel and Gretel were so terrified that they let fall what they had in their hands. The old woman, however, nodded her head and said, 'Oh, you dear children, who has brought you here? Do come in, and stay with me. No harm shall happen to you.' She took them into her little house, and good food was set before them. Afterwards, two pretty little beds were covered with clean white linen, and Hansel and Gretel lay down in them, and thought they were in heaven.

'Look at the pi'ture,' Larry said, pointing at the plate.

'What do you see?'

'She's like the Mammy. She's older, but look at them ear-rings. And see them shoes she's a-wearin'. It's her a'righ'. That there's the Mammy.'

It has been a custom in visual representations of fairy-tales that the criminal, be it male or female (and in fairy-tales the human representation of evil tends to be female, while the male representation tends to be an anthropo-morphic beast – the big bad wolf or the troll or a demonic dwarf), is often depicted as being physically similar to the parent of that sex. This continues right up to J. M. Barrie's Peter Pan. Captain Hook is the double of Mr Darling, Wendy's father. It's hard to know if this is a modern, Freudian interpretation of a child's fear of their parents, or if it was ever intended by the early storytellers. It's probably a moot point, though, since it is another element that has been dropped by present-day publishers.

'Yes, I think that she is very like the Mammy.'

'No, she *is* the Mammy!'

'Is that what you think?'

'Yeah. She be's a witch, don' she?'

'Will I read the next bit?'

'Yeah.'

The old woman had only pretended to be so kind, she was in reality a wicked witch, who lay in wait for children, and had only built the little bread house in order to entice them there. When a child fell into her power, she killed it, cooked and ate it, and that was a feast day with her. Witches have red eyes and cannot see far, but they have a keen scent like the beasts, and are aware when human beings draw near. When Hansel and Gretel came into her neighbourhood, she laughed maliciously, and said mockingly, 'I have them, they shall not escape me again!'

'Yeah, she does be a witch a'righ'. That ol'Mammy was a witch all the time, so she was. I knowed it.'

'Why did you think that?'

''Cause she was so mean, and made the Daddy do what she wanted and he done it, even though he din'hate them kids like she done.'

'You don't think the Daddy was that mean, then?'

'No, the Mammy is worse. That's why she does be a witch. If she hadn' bin there, that ol' Daddy prob'ly woulda bin nice 'nough to them there kidses.'

'You seem pretty sure about that.'

'Oh, I know what Mammies is like. They's much worser than what Daddies is. That ol'Daddy, him's not a bad ol' fella really. I tink him's ascairt of 'er, tha's the problem.'

'But he's bigger than her. Why would he be afraid of her, Larry?'

The boy looked solemnly at the plate, and pointed to the figure of the witch, standing at her doorway in the forest glade where the bread house acted as a beacon for lost children.

'Lookit 'er. See that there face? She lookens small an' weak an' old, but she idn't. Inside of her she's stronger and wickeder than any man. See how them there kidses is lookin' at 'er? See how scairt they is? They see wha' she really do be like. They *know*. She tricksies 'em with her voice, 'tendses to be all nice. But right there, when they

196

sees 'er for the first time, they knows. They knows she's mean and cruel.'

'Can you tell just by looking at someone that they're mean or cruel?'

He was still gazing, rapt, at the painting in the book.

'Oh, yeah, wit some people you can. I knowed wit . . .' His voice tapered off.

'Who, Larry? Who did you know who was like that?'

He shook his head vigorously, as if there were flies inside it that he was trying to quell.

'No. I can' say. She'll find out if I telled.'

'You can tell me, Larry. No one can get you here.'

'She can. She ain' 'fraid o' nobody. She tole me that if I ever said the tings she done, she'd get me. I'm fierce scairt of her, so I am.'

'Okay. We can talk about it when you're ready. Will I finish the story?'

But he stood up, looking distressed, glancing at the window as if expecting to see a wizened face pressed against the glass.

'No. I wan't' go t' my room. I don' wan' no more tonight.'

'Okay, Larry. Want me to go up with you?'

He shook his head and backed cautiously from the room, his eyes fixed on the window all the time. I sat alone in the silence and flicked through the last few pages, looking at the plates in the remainder of the book. I paused on a scene of the witch stoking the oven to roast Hansel. The lines of her face were thrown into sharp relief by the light of the flickering embers, her visage a rictus of spite and menace. The image was so vivid it made me shudder.

Who was the witch in Larry's life? The only real possibility was difficult to countenance, and cast an even more unpleasant pallor on the Byrnes' story. It also led me into the realms of a societal taboo that was rarely talked about, even in child protection.

I stood up and looked through the window and across the lawn at the high trees of the overgrown garden behind Rivendell, as a cloud of crows came in to roost and the darkness caught the city in its embrace.

PART THREE

Hard Times

Let us pause in life's pleasures
And count its many tears
As we all sup sorrow with the poor.
There's a song that will linger for ever in our ears:
Hard times, come again no more.

'Tis the song, the sigh of the weary:
Hard times, hard times – come again no more.
Many days you have lingered, around my cabin door.
Hard times, come again no more.

Hard Times BY STEPHEN FOSTER
(FROM THE SINGING OF WOODY GUTHRIE)

The piercing sound of my mobile phone ringing cut through fragrant clouds of sleep and brought me to jarring consciousness. I swore loudly and fumbled about on the bedside locker until my hand fell on the jangling, flashing irritant. It was just getting bright outside, which meant it was sometime around five in the morning.

'What?'

'Shane, it's Ben. Did I wake you?'

'No. I was up practising my Tai Chi.'

'Good for you. Mina Henry is missing again. She apparently found out the alarm codes of the house, used them and strolled out the front door some time during the night.'

'She's run before. Why the hell are you ringing me at the crack of dawn?'

'She left a note this time. It says she's not coming back. Her parents are distraught, and have been asking for you.'

'The last time I was there, they threw me out. Tell them they can fucking wait until a civilized hour.'

'Shane, the note she left could be construed as suicidal.'

I lay there, the phone pressed to my ear, staring at the ceiling. I noticed a thin wisp of spider-web filigreed around the light fixture. Was Mina suicidal? She was certainly upset. Possibly depressed. Definitely angry.

I couldn't risk it.

'I'll get over there, see what the story is.'

'Okay. Call me if you need anything.'

'I could do with a cup of coffee right about now.'

'Can't help you there. Call me.'

I put the phone down and rolled out of bed. Coffee would have to wait.

It would prove to be a very long day.

Molly put a cafetière of aromatic coffee and one of her ridiculous, tiny bone-china cups and saucers down on the kitchen table in front of me. I was reading Mina's note. It wasn't heartening, but I would have been lying had I said that its contents surprised me.

Dear Mum and Dad,

I cannot stay here any more. I have tried but you want me to be somebody and something that I am just not. I am not happy and I am making you not happy as well. Sorry.

I have thought about it and thought about it. There does not seem to be any place that I feel right. I just don't fit. You always treated me like I could do anything, as long as it was something you wanted me to do. If it was something I wanted but you did not, you put something in the way and that was that. I am tired of fighting. I never win anyway.

I am going away now and I am not coming back. Thank you for loving me. I know you did, the best way you could. I wanted to be the daughter you would have liked. But I am just not that person. Take good care of one another.

Love,

Mina

I put the letter, written in Mina's precise hand on a lined page from a copybook, down on the table, depressed the plunger of the cafetière and poured myself a thimbleful. It was extremely good, and welcome. Pity I'd have to refill my cup every thirty seconds or so, but perhaps I was just being picky.

Dirk was dressed in full executive regalia, but his eyes were red and he looked gaunt. Molly was in a long, kimono-looking dressing gown that went from her ankles to her neck. On her feet she wore oriental-style slippers. They looked authentic, if not comfortable.

'Well,' Dirk said, 'any thoughts?'

I knew that he was fighting to keep himself under control. There was a part of me that felt he deserved the pain he was obviously feeling. It wasn't like I hadn't warned them both that this was coming. But a larger portion felt sorry for him, for them both. Just like Mina, they had not been able to change who they were. They would have to, if we were to drag this back from the edge of disaster.

'I would not read this as a suicide note.'

He and Molly visibly sagged with relief.

'Thank God,' Dirk said, rubbing his eyes. 'I didn't think so, but she's been so down.'

'She's at a low ebb, there's no doubt of that. But I don't think she's at risk of killing herself. She's *got* something to live for.'

They both looked at me.

'Jacob Benedict,' Molly said, deadpan.

'Yes. She loves him, Molly. Unequivocally. You've tried to quash it. You've told her to forget him. You've banned her from seeing him. All you have succeeded in doing is turning him into a fantasy, an image of all the things she wants but can't have. They have discussed marriage. There's a whole scenario they've created for themselves: where they'll live, what work they'll do . . . she's seventeen, he's not much older; the likelihood of them remaining together is slim, but all this adversity has pushed them closer. You need to give them a chance to try.'

Dirk looked at Molly, then back at me. He cleared his throat and straightened his tie.

'Can you find her?'

'I have no idea. But I'll try. How long has she been gone?'

'She keyed in the alarm code at 12.30 a.m., according to the machine's computer.'

'If I bring her back, will you allow her to see Jacob? There's not much point if you don't. She'll just go again, and each time she'll find somewhere better to hide. And, while she's not a suicide risk now, that doesn't mean she can't become one. And there are many other risks where she's going. I won't bullshit you, I am worried about her.'

'We'll facilitate them in pursuing their relationship,' Dirk said quietly. 'I just want my daughter back. I want to see her smile again. I want her to look at me like she used to: with love, not accusation in her eyes. You were right. I'm man enough to say it. You were right, and I'm sorry. But, please, use all your resources to bring her back to me. To us.'

I poured my tenth cup of coffee, drained it and stood up.

'I'm going to go home, to get a shower and some breakfast. Then, when the rest of the world wakes up, I'll go and look for her. There's still the chance she'll come home by herself. I don't think it's likely, but I wouldn't write it off completely.'

'Just find her,' Molly said. 'Please.'

'I'll do my best. But it's very hard to find someone who doesn't want to be found.'

Jacob didn't know where she was.

I was over at the workshop, which seemed to be the most sensible place to begin. I sat with him in their canteen. Ellen was beside him. Brendan beside her. Nobody had any ideas, and nobody developed any while I was there. Jacob had his head bowed, refusing to look at anyone.

'I ain't seen her. Not since she stopped comin' here. You *know* that, 'cause I told you a few days ago.'

'I was just wondering if she had been in touch with you. She's run away from home again, Jacob, and I'm trying to find her. Her mum and dad have told me that they don't mind you two being boyfriend and girlfriend, just so long as she comes home.'

'They say that now 'cause they wants her to come back. They don't mean it.'

'I think they do, this time.'

He shrugged and continued to stare at the table.

'I think that's all you're going to get here, Shane,' Brendan said, sweat glistening on his brow. The back of his shirt was plastered to his back. It was just nine thirty, and I wondered what kind of condition he'd be in by midday. 'You can run along, Jacob. Thanks for your help.'

Jacob stood up and walked briskly from the room without looking back.

'There. Are you satisfied, Shane?' Brendan said, trying to look smug and not succeeding. 'I told you you'd get nothing from him. He's a morose young man, at the best of times. I don't know where you got the idea that he and Mina had a connection. They rarely even look at one another here.'

'They're putting on a performance, Brendan, that's why they don't seem to be close,' I said, feeling tired. 'He's angry, now, angry as hell. He came to me, I told him I'd help him and I've let him and Mina down.'

'Aren't you overstating things?' Ellen said. 'I'm not sure they're capable of the kind of sneaking around you're suggesting.'

I stood up, shaking my head. 'Will you call me if you hear anything?'

Brendan and Ellen nodded, looking at one another in bewilderment.

At eleven thirty I was standing at the bar of The Sailing Cot. The same barman told me categorically that he had not seen Mina, and that she would not be welcome if he did. I left him my number and asked him to call me if she showed up, but I wasn't confident. I hadn't made any friends on my last visit.

I left the bar and walked back to where the Austin nestled against the high edge of the footpath. I leant against the bonnet and lit my fifteenth cigarette of the day, realizing that, for all my good intentions, I was out of ideas. My only two reasonable avenues of enquiry were Jacob and the dingy bar behind me. I could trawl through the rest of the dives in the city, but that would take weeks, and would probably result in nothing. Mina had spent the night somewhere, and something told me that she hadn't slept rough. The thin man I had met her with before was probably one of a network of contacts she had in the strange underworld to which she fled. I needed someone else who knew their way around this grim landscape. I knew someone who fitted the bill, but I was reluctant to contact him. You never knew what can of worms you would be opening up when you asked for his services. He was unorthodox and spectacularly unpredictable. But I was out of serviceable options. I took my mobile from my pocket, and pulled a number out of the phonebook.

'Can I speak to Devereux?'

Karl Devereux is a Community Worker from Blackalley, an area not unlike Haroldstown, but on the other side of the city and possibly more troubled. So far as I could tell from the complex mythology that has sprung up about him, Devereux was born to an alcoholic mother who never saw him as anything other than a burden. He did not know who his father was, and fell in with a youth gang when he was eight years old. Graduating from runner to gang enforcer by the time he was sixteen, he went free-lance in his twenties, working for several criminal enterprises as well as a certain republican terrorist organization whenever they required his particular skills in the Republic. He was without the restriction of any kind of political ideology or any discernible qualms of morality, which made him an extremely sought-after professional in his particular field: general thuggery of all kinds, with a bit of shooting and explosives work thrown in for good measure.

Eventually, when his career was at its height, Devereux was arrested, more than likely through information tendered by a jealous competitor. Evidence had been planted at a crime scene; testimony was given by a previous employer who happened to be behind bars and wished to alleviate his sentence; Devereux went down. The crime he was convicted of (and he never for a second said that he didn't do it – he refused, in fact, to say anything at all throughout his trial) had been carried out for a private operator, and since he was not actually a member of the IRA, he got none of the privileges of a prisoner of war. The Good Friday Agreement did him no favours. He served his time with common criminals, and he did it quietly and without trouble. He had enough of a reputation to be feared, and therefore was left alone. But prison had other effects on him.

Irish prisons are not pleasant places. Mountjoy, which is where Devereux did the bulk of his time, is a foul, overcrowded, inhuman institution, well known for its high incidence of drug addiction, for the mindless violence that seems to be so commonplace within its walls and for the regular suicide attempts of its inmates. It is not known for its ability to rehabilitate career criminals. Yet Devereux came out a changed man.

No one really knows what happened to him in Mountjoy. He served eight years of a ten-year sentence and nothing earth-shattering happened during that time. There were a couple of riots in 'The Joy', in none of which he participated. He worked for a time in the laundry, had responsibility for the prison library for two years, and is said to have conducted himself competently, but without distinction, at these tasks. He took a course in Sociology and another in Irish History, through the Prison Education Scheme, although he did not sit exams for either. I have spoken to the tutors of these courses, and they tell me that Devereux rarely spoke up in class, but that when he did he displayed a level of comprehension far above that of the other students, and would certainly have achieved certification in the higher percentiles. It has been suggested that he found Jesus, but he was not seen to regularly attend the prison chapel, and the Catholic chaplain is on the record as stating that he never had a single conversation with the quiet, dark-eyed man whom the other prisoners tended to steer clear of.

Whatever occurred, Devereux emerged from the walls of Ireland's toughest penal institution a reformed character. He returned to Blackalley, and gradually began to do voluntary work for the Community Services in the area where he had grown up: assisting in the running of youth clubs; helping out with Meals on Wheels; doing outreach work with prostitutes; driving buses for the Irish Wheelchair Association; working night-shifts at the homeless shelter – and never accepting a penny for any of it, despite being offered full-time posts with several local organizations. He seemed to enjoy the freedom of being a freelancer (a remnant, possibly, of his earlier incarnation) and, while he worked out of an office in the main community centre, he continued to live off social welfare and spread his interests among the local voluntary groups, all of whom welcomed him as a much needed pair of hands. Devereux never hid his history, wore it like a badge of honour, in fact. Here was a man who had been there, had come up on the very streets where he now worked, taken the dark road, paid for it, and was now going to give something back.

Karl Devereux was maybe forty years old, with long black hair, combed straight back, and an angular, clean-shaven face. He was dressed in jeans, a denim shirt and a grey, light linen jacket. He wore no rings or watch, and his shoes, which I could see because he had them propped up on his office desk, were plain black leather. There was not a pick of spare flesh on him, and, when he moved, which was only when he had to, it was with the grace of a dancer. His eyes were a cold, pale blue.

I finished telling him about Mina, and he nodded, slowly.

'She hasn't returned? You've checked with her parents?' His voice was without accent, deep and rich.

'I called them just before I arrived. They haven't heard from her.'

'You said she's run before. Is this the longest she's been away?'

'I think so. It's usually just overnight.'

He nodded again, but I could tell he was elsewhere, running over possibilities in his head. He had an encyclopaedic knowledge of the city, particularly the parts most others did not know.

'There are several things that spring to mind.'

'So you'll help me?'

He nodded as he continued speaking. 'There is a market for young girls of her . . . appearance . . . there are those who will pay handsomely for them. She may already have been taken to be trafficked out of the country.'

'It's never happened before. I think she goes to the same people each time she runs away from home. They're probably using her, but I don't think she's in danger of being taken out of the country.'

'Let's hope not, but it's sensible to be prepared for every eventuality. Her people are wealthy?'

'Yes.'

'There are those who would find her, if her father was prepared to pay for it. I could give him some names of reliable men.'

'You mean mercenaries or private investigators.'

'People who know how to do that kind of work, yes.'

'Well, if we fail, that may just be something to consider.'

Devereux stood up in a fluid motion – one moment he was sitting with his legs up on the desk, the next he was standing with his hand outstretched.

'If she's still in the city, I'll find her. Should it turn out that she's been moved, I know people who can find her, as there's money to be had for doing it. Tell her family not to worry.'

I shook his hand, which was very dry to the touch.

'I wish there really was nothing to worry about, Devereux. I honestly do.'

He smiled, which actually looked sort of sad.

'She's undoubtedly in danger. But we'll bring her back.'

After that, it's up to them to help her sort through whatever it is that's causing her pain. And she'll have to do some work herself. There's only so much others can do for her. Ultimately, it'll be up to her.'

I walked to the door of his small office.

'Call me as soon as you've got anything.'

'When I've found her, you'll know.'

'Don't pick her up without me. She'll need a familiar face.'

'As you wish.'

I walked through the main office and out to the car-park, wondering what I'd unleashed.

It was early afternoon when I finished with Devereux, and, after ringing the Henrys to inform them of my (lack of) progress, I drove over to Haroldstown to see the Walshes. I was due a visit, and, on a more selfish note, I wanted to do something that would take my mind off Mina and her plight.

I had decided that I would act on Benjamin's advice and stop beating about the bush, surreptitiously attempting to build a case for or against the reality or unreality of the haunting. I was going to approach the issue head-on.

When I got to the house, I called Biddy aside.

'I want to go out the back with the boys today, Biddy. We've played games around this for long enough. I want to see what goes on out there.'

'I've told you before, I don't want that.'

We were standing in the dark hallway. I could hear the sound of the television from the living room, a cartoon playing loudly.

'Do you want me to help them, Biddy?'

She looked at her shoes, a battle clearly going on in her face.

'All right, don't do anything to scare him, okay?'

'I promise I'm not going to cause a fuss. It doesn't really matter whether I believe in what's happening in the garden or not. What matters is what it's doing to your sons. I want to see how they are when they're with him.'

She nodded and gestured towards the door of the living room. 'Go and do what you have to do.'

Bobby and Micky gave me a warm welcome, chatting excitedly about a trip they had taken with their mother and aunt to the park the day before. I looked at some pictures they had drawn for me of them on the swings and slides (I had been encouraging them to record as much of their lives as possible through a variety of media) and then I agreed to watch the rest of the cartoon with them before we began the session.

When the cartoon had finished, I switched off the box, and we sat down on the floor, facing each other.

'I want to meet your dad today, boys. I'd like you to bring me out with you, and introduce me. I think it's time. We've talked a lot about him. Now maybe you can show me.'

They looked at me gravely, then at each other.

'He don'just come. He calls to us when he wants to see us,' Bobby said. 'He might not come for you.'

'He calls to me,' Micky said firmly.

'Well, can't you call him? Won't he come if you want him to?'

'S'pose we could try,' Bobby said, looking uncertain.

'I'd really like it if you did.'

Micky was already on his feet. 'C'mon then. I think I should be the one. He calls me, see? I'll do it, righ'?'

Bobby sat where he was for a moment, seemingly still unsure of the proposed enterprise.

'Does Mammy know 'bout this?'

'Yes. I asked her if it was okay.'

'I don' tink Daddy will be too happy.'

'Why not?'

He shook his head, obviously unhappy. 'I jus' don't. Le's play a game instead. What 'bout musical chairs? We played that th' other time. It was good fun, wasn' it?'

Micky was at the door by now.

'Oh, come on, Bob. It'll be okay. Stop bein' a sissy.'

Begrudgingly, Bobby stood up and followed us.

They walked down the narrow path that ran through the grass lawn that covered most of the garden, and stepped up onto the raised verge of the ditch, which was overhung with branches from trees and shrubs that had grown wild behind it. I remained several feet from them, not wanting to get in the way, squatted down on my haunches and waited. The object of the exercise was not to intervene. I simply wanted to see what happened during these secret meetings.

They stood for a few seconds, not saying anything. I got the sense that they were gauging the atmosphere, taking stock of the light and the temperature. Micky was slowly turning in circles, looking at the top of the tree line. Finally, after several minutes had passed, he called loudly: 'Daddy! Daddy, I wants you. Daddy, come and see us, please.'

I had expected that he would continue calling, but after that single cry he fell quiet, and he and his brother stood side by side on the ditch and waited.

What happened next has played on my mind a good deal in the intervening years, and I wish to state clearly that I am open to admitting that there may have been aspects of suggestion in how I perceived it. But, as far as I can recall, and without conscious exaggeration, this is what I experienced with those two children that summer's afternoon.

Everything seemed to go very still, as if the trees had stopped all movement and the very breath of the wind had ceased. I felt a trickle of sweat run down the small of my back. It was as if the actual environment was subdued, waiting pensively for someone or something.

'He's coming,' Micky said.

A sudden blast of cold wind almost knocked me over and I had to steady myself with a hand on the ground. The branches over the children's heads lashed violently and then, just as quickly, were still, but a very audible breeze continued to ruffle the leaves like an electric current.

'Hello, Daddy,' Bobby said, his eyes now fixed on that intangible point in the air.

'Daddy, this is Shane – he's our friend we told you 'bout,' Micky said, and I noticed that there was a new quality to his voice. It seemed to be deeper.

The boys went quiet, seemingly listening to something. I moved slowly around to the left, trying desperately to see if they were using a visual point of reference, but once again could see nothing.

'Daddy, that isn't nice,' Bobby said. 'He's not bad. He's good to us.'

Micky had started to look frightened. I had to fight the urge to go to him. Something was happening. And whatever it was, they were unprepared for it.

'I don't wanna say that to him, Daddy,' Micky said. 'He's my friend.'

'That's not true. He wouldn't do that,' Bobby said, tears in his voice now.

I'd had enough. I stood up and slowly walked over to them. They were apparently unaware of me, locked into the confrontation with whomever or whatever it was they could see. I reached out my hand and touched Bobby on the arm. He started, pulling away from me in alarm.

'You gotta go 'way from here,' he said, his body quaking. 'Not in the house – far 'way. He's awful mad. You gotta go right now.'

'What's going on, Bob?' I asked, trying to sound calm, but probably not succeeding. The air seemed to be full of electricity. I could almost see it crackling about us. A bank of dark clouds had gathered overhead, and there was a scent of rain heavy in the air.

Micky slowly turned his head so that he was looking at me. His eyes were bloodshot, his pupils dilated to the point that I could barely see the corneas.

'He says he hurted you once before,' he droned in a monotone. 'To show you he was real. You gots to go now, or he'll hurt you again. Worser. He don't want you in the house no more.'

The wind kicked up again, a plaintive wailing accompanying it. In a great downward gush, the rain came. I was soaked through in seconds.

'Come on, boys,' I shouted over the roar of the elements, pulling both of them to me. 'It's time to go back in.'

They came passively, moving as if they were in a trance. I closed the back door against the howling gale and ferocious downpour, and steered the boys to the front of the house. I could hear Biddy moving about upstairs. She did not come down to join us. Bobby and Micky sat together on the couch, staring at the wall.

'You gots to go,' Bobby said again, shivering, water running from his hair into his eyes. 'He ain't goin' to let you stay.'

I sat down in front of them on the floor, placing a hand on each one's shoulder.

'I'm not going anywhere,' I said firmly. 'He can't hurt me, and he won't.'

Micky, a strand of saliva dangling from his lower lip, stifled a sob. 'You don't know him. He's mad now, and that means trouble for you. Don't make him mad no more.'

I looked out the window, and was amazed to see the sun shining brightly, and not a single raindrop on the glass pane. The boys and I were drenched. I stood up and went to the front door, opening it. The footpaths were bone dry. Somehow, it had rained at the back of the house, but not at the front.

I went home and changed into dry clothes, then sat in front of the TV for half an hour, channel surfing. I opened a bottle of beer, but took a couple of sips and set it aside. I switched off the television and put on a CD, Springsteen's *Nebraska*.

I grabbed my keys and went back out.

It was six when I knocked on the door of Sylvie's flat. The front door of the building had been opened by a skinny woman who was coming out as I walked up, and she let me in without even looking at me.

There was no response, so I banged a bit more loudly, calling: 'Sylvie, it's Shane. Are you home?'

She opened the door, and I felt my heart drop.

She'd been badly beaten. Her left eye was swollen shut, her cheek on that side red and puffy. Her lower lip had obviously burst, probably through her having bitten it, and it was caked in blood, misshapen and discoloured. Her forehead was black and grazed. I could see more marks about her neck and shoulder, where her top hung loose. The rest of her was probably a patchwork of bruises too.

'Have you come to see your handiwork?' she asked.

'Oh Christ, Sylvie, I'm sorry.' I knew why this had happened, and I felt sick to my stomach.

She turned and walked back into the flat. 'He hasn't been back since, so you may as well come in. Mind you, what you were thinkin' comin' at this time, when he's usually here, I don't know.'

I followed her inside and closed the door behind me.

'He did this because of what I said to him?'

The flat was a mess. It had been spotlessly tidy on my last visit. It seemed that she had let things slide. The room was in semi-darkness, the curtains drawn. Toys, rumpled clothes, cups, plates, dirty nappies rolled up in balls, used baby-wipes were everywhere. The television was on with the sound muted, playing *The Simpsons*. The door to the kitchen was open, and I could see that it was in an advanced state of disarray too. The smell of rancid food seeped out.

'From what he told me, you did a little more than talk to him. He said you tried to rough him up.'

I plonked down onto the couch.

'I may have gotten a little physical, but I didn't hit him or anything. He wasn't hurt.'

'It doesn't matter. He's beat me up before plenty of times.'

She was a wreck in more ways than just the injuries. Her hair was stuck to her head, greasy from days without being washed. Her clothes were wrinkled and stained. I could smell sweat and more from where I was sitting. She obviously hadn't been looking after herself.

'It doesn't excuse it. If I caused this to happen, I'm truly sorry. I was trying to get him to treat you better, not worse.'

She attempted to smile and stopped, her lip causing her pain.

'He said that you'd made it so's he couldn't pimp me out any more. Said that if he couldn't put me on the street, then he might as well have me for himself. So he had his fun with me and then gave me a fairly sound hidin'. Usually, when he beats me, he tries not to leave any marks. This time, he didn't have to worry about that.'

'So I see.'

'Then, he left. Just like that. I haven't seen or heard from him since.'

'D'you think he's gone? I mean, has he left you for prolonged periods before?'

She shook her head. 'Never. I'd be fuckin' thrilled except that I've no money, and we're out of food and Gloria needs nappies and formula. We're pretty screwed, to be honest. I woulda gone out to work anyways, except the woman downstairs won't take the baby. Daddy told her not to.'

'Well, I can help you there. I'll pop down the shops and get some groceries and stuff for the baby. Why don't I cook us dinner? I haven't eaten yet. What do you say?'

'Kitchen's a bit of a mess,' she said sheepishly, sounding every bit the thirteen-year-old she was.

'Well, it's nothing a little cleaning and tidying won't fix. Where's Gloria now?'

'Asleep in her cot.'

'Will she be okay while I pop out and you hop in the shower?'

'Yeah. I can leave the door open in case she wakes up.'

'Good. Get yourself cleaned up. Put on some fresh clothes. I'll be about half an hour. Is there anything in particular you'd like to eat?'

'Anything?'

'Sure. Whatever you like.'

She thought for a second.

'In the centre, they used to make us sausage and mash on a Monday. Today's Monday, isn't it?'

'All day.'

'Can you make that?'

'I think my culinary abilities can stretch that far. Go on. Get yourself looking human again. I'll see you in a bit.'

I felt as if I had beaten her myself. I couldn't believe I had been so stupid, that my macho need to protect her had clouded my judgement so badly. There was nothing to be gained from dwelling on it just then, so I did my waste-paper basket exercise again, and went to the car. I decided to focus on the mundane, on shopping, cleaning and cooking for her. I thought that, if I could immerse myself in the nuts-and-bolts of everyday living, I could get through the evening without becoming so consumed by guilt that I ceased to be functional.

There was a supermarket ten minutes up the road. I got a trolley and did a week's worth of a shop, getting basics like bread, milk and butter, as well as some fresh fruit and vegetables, tins of beans, peas and soup, dried pasta and rice. I threw in some frozen meals, unsure of how competent a cook Sylvie was, and plenty of baby products: nappies, formula, lotion, talcum-powder, as well as some of those jars of baby-food. I planned to check back in on her regularly anyway, and would need to talk to her about her financial situation. There were allowances she was entitled to, but the authorities would ask questions about her age and ability to care for Gloria. We had some serious conversations ahead of us, and Sylvie wasn't going to like any of them.

I stopped off at a chemist on the way back and bought painkillers and antiseptic cream, plasters and bandages. The cuts and bruises looked painful, and it didn't seem that she had made any effort to tend to them.

She let me in, dressed in a black T-shirt and jeans, flip-flops on her feet. Her short hair was tousled and she had a towel draped round her shoulders. I dumped the groceries in the centre of the living-room floor and handed the bag from the chemist to her.

'I want you to take care of those bruises,' I said, 'while I clean up the kitchen and get dinner on. Then we'll tackle the rest of this place. If we get stuck in, it'll be done by the time the food's ready.'

She nodded. Now that she'd washed, her face didn't look so bad. I guessed that she hadn't bothered with personal hygiene since he'd given her the beating, and the blood had congealed, making it look worse than it actually was.

The kitchen, on the other hand, was every bit as bad as it looked. I stacked dishes, scraping the contents into one of the plastic bags from the groceries, and ran some hot water into the sink, leaving the crockery to steep for a few minutes as I tidied up jars and sauce-bottles that had been left sitting among the crumbs and sticky knives and forks on the small kitchen table. I had bought detergent and dishcloths, and gave all the surfaces a good scrubbing, then went to work on the contents of the sink.

When the kitchen was reasonably clean and tidy, I packed away the groceries I had bought, then peeled potatoes and put them on to boil. As I was chopping an onion for the gravy, Sylvie stuck her head in the door. She looked even better, having cleaned out the cut on her lip and stuck a plaster on the grazing on her cheekbone.

'Anything I can do?'

I pointed to the pile of empty plastic bags.

'I've got things under control in here. Why don't you make a start on the living room? I've been using those as rubbish bags.'

She smiled, took a couple and ducked out. Seconds later I heard her opening the curtains. She seemed more upbeat, and I reasoned that she was as happy to be doing something – anything – as I was. I like to cook, and the simple rhythms of making a meal acted as a kind of non-chemical anaesthetic.

I heated a frying pan, drizzled in a little olive oil and put on the sausages. When they had browned, I removed them, putting them on a plate and leaving them in the warmed oven. I threw the chopped onions onto the pan, letting them soften in the remaining oil and then tossing in some butter, salt and black pepper. I left them to simmer.

'D'you have a vacuum cleaner?' I called to Sylvie.

'Yeah. It's in the press there in the kitchen.'

I brought it into the living room and plugged it into the wall socket.

'Will this wake Gloria?'

'Probably, but it's time she woke anyway. Our routine's all shot to shit these past few days. I haven't known which way was up. If she wakes, she wakes.'

I nodded, and switched on the power with my foot. Sylvie had a duster and was cleaning the screen of the TV.

When the place was liveable in again, I put the vacuum cleaner back in its place, and checked the potatoes. They were done. I poured off the water, retaining it in a bowl to use for the gravy. I made the mash with butter, salt, nutmeg and milk. Sylvie laid the table as I added the stock to the onions, deglazed the pan, then added some flour and mustard to make the gravy.

'Jesus, that smells great,' she said, looking over my shoulder.

'Hungry?'

'Fuckin' starvin'. The cupboard's been bare for a while.'

'Well, hand me those plates. Watch out, they're hot.'

Just as we were setting the food on the table, Gloria began to make waking noises from the bedroom, and Sylvie went in and got her. I put some potato into a bowl for the baby, cooling it with some milk, and added a little of the gravy for flavour. Sylvie changed her nappy, gave her a quick wash, and we sat to eat.

Sylvie didn't say much during the meal, but she ate two helpings, allowing me to feed Gloria, who seemed to enjoy it almost as much as her mother. She was a happy, smiling child, gurgling merrily to herself, and, despite my best efforts, she managed to get food pretty much all over herself and no small amount on me. I had bought some Ben and Jerry's cookie-dough ice-cream for dessert, and we took it into the living room. The sound of the street came in through the open windows, and Sylvie put a CD into a small player she had.

'The Carpenters?' I said in surprise as the first chords of *Close to You* played.

'Shut up. I like 'em.'

'Not a damn thing wrong with the Carpenters.'

'Me 'n' Gloria love this song. Don't we, Gloria?'

The baby, who was sitting on the floor playing with a stuffed bear almost as big as herself, looked up at the sound of her name and smiled, burbling something at us.

'I never would have seen you as a Carpenters' kind of girl.'

'And what kind of girl would you have seen me as?'

'I dunno. Chart stuff. Britney Spears, Beyoncé; Westlife, maybe.'

'Well now, you're wrong as can be. I don't like any of that shit. I like the Carpenters and I *love* Simon and Garfunkel. And Elvis, of course.'

'You're full of surprises.'

She sat in an armchair and attacked her ice-cream.

'So how'd you get into the Carpenters? They don't exactly get blanket airplay on the radio. At least not lately anyway.'

'D'you remember Yolanda? At the centre?'

'Yolanda Frears? Yeah.'

'Yolanda was my key-worker for a few years. She used to listen to the Carpenters and Simon and Garfunkel. And my daddy likes Elvis.'

'I see.'

She gazed off into space as Karen Carpenter sang about how the angels came together and decided to create a dream come true.

'It's a happy song, I think,' she said, 'but she still sounds sort of sad. It doesn't matter what she's singing about. She always sounds that way.'

'She wasn't a very happy person, Sylvie. She died very young. Starved herself to death. Anorexia, y'know? Happy people don't do that.'

'I didn't know.'

'It doesn't make the music any less beautiful.'

'More, maybe. Poor Mrs Carpenter. I wonder what she was sad about.'

'I don't know. I haven't read a whole lot about them, to be honest. Saw a movie about them when I was a teenager, but I don't remember much about it.'

'That's okay.'

The food had made Sylvie drowsy. I left her sitting with her eyes partially closed, listening to the music, and did the washing up. When I'd dried up and put the crockery and cutlery away, I came back into the living room to find her fast asleep. I looked at Gloria, who was still engrossed by the bear.

'Well, it's just you and me, kiddo,' I said in a whisper.

I played quietly with the child for an hour or so. The quality of light coming in through the windows changed slowly to golden and then a deep red. Gloria began to yawn too, and I made her up a bottle and changed her nappy. She fell asleep on my knee finishing her formula and I brought her into the cot in one of the small bedrooms and covered her over.

I went over to the CD player. She seemed to have only three albums: greatest hits from the Carpenters, Elvis, and Simon and Garfunkel. I put Simon and Garfunkel on, and went to the open window to smoke a cigarette.

Sylvie stirred into wakefulness as Art Garfunkel was singing *For Emily, Wherever I May Find Her*.

'What do you think he's singing about?' she asked, her voice still thick with sleep.

'I always thought he was singing about a girl he loved. I don't think the words make much sense really. They're pretty, though.'

'Do you have a girl?'

'Yes.'

'Do you love her?'

'I do.'

'Does she love you?'

'Yeah, I think she does.'

'Why aren't you with her now?'

'She doesn't live in the city. She has a job somewhere else.'

'D'you miss her?'

'Sometimes.'

The sun was sinking over the rooftops outside, the room dark, now. I felt tired suddenly. *How could I help this child? Was I fooling myself into thinking I could save her when she was so very far gone?* I pushed the feeling aside and flicked the butt out of the window. We needed to talk about the future. The conversation could wait no longer.

'Enjoy your sleep?'

She nodded. 'Where's Gloria?'

'In her cot. I gave her a bottle and changed her, and she conked out. She was no bother.'

'She never is.'

'Sylvie, we need to talk about what you're going to do.'

'I know.'

'Have you thought about it, at all?'

'Of course I have.'

'And?'

'Can't I stay here? I don't think he's comin' back. He kept sayin' how you'd messed it all up for him. How he'd never have any peace here now. I could sign on the dole, or somethin'.'

'You're too young to get the dole, pet. You'd get Lone Parent's Allowance, I think, but even then questions would be asked. We're going to have to bring in the Health Services, I'm afraid. Look, I know some people. I promise you that I will not allow them to take Gloria away. There are places where you can both live and where you'll get support.'

'I can do it myself, Shane. I don't want to go back into care. I can manage.'

'No, you can't. Look at the condition you were in when I got here. And you would have gone back out to the street. That temptation will always be there, and you need to learn other ways of coping. Your father *may* come back, and what then? We have to make sure that you're completely safe.'

'Shane.' She was crying now. I couldn't see the tears in the half-light, but I could hear them. 'I've been fucked by the system before. I know that I can't live like this, and I don't want to. But I can't go back into care either. I just can't. I don't know what to do.'

I went over to her and took her hands in mine. 'I left you before, Sylvie, and I'm sorry. I won't again. I give you my word that I will not let anything happen to you. I'm going to get you a phone, with my number on speed-dial, and you can call me at any time and I will be there. I work with a man who can help us to find somewhere that's just right for you and Gloria. I'll talk to him tomorrow and we'll start looking. It'll work out, I swear.'

She lost control of the tears. 'Oh God, help me. Please help me. I can't do this any more.'

I put my arms around her and let her cry. The sobs

racked her small frame as nearly fourteen years of pain and loss finally bubbled to the surface. There was nothing I could do but let her pour it all out, and I knelt there on the tatty carpet in the darkness and held her.

It seemed to go on for a long time. Finally she said: 'Sorry.'

'What for?'

'Being such a dork.'

'That's okay. It's nothing to be ashamed of.'

'I'll go where you tell me to go. I don't have much other choice, do I?'

'There are always choices, honey. That's something you need to learn. The trick is to know the right one when you see it. That'll be something for both of us to work on. We need to find the best option for you and that little girl in there. We'll work on it together, with my boss, and we'll get it right, I promise. And if we don't, we'll try something else, and we'll keep trying until we *do* get it right.'

'Do you swear? Cross you heart and hope to die?'

'Cross my heart.'

'Okay then.'

My legs were cramping, but I stayed where I was. She was pressed tight into me, her fingers digging into my shoulders in a fierce grip.

'Why are you helping me?' she whispered, her face against my hair.

I considered my answer carefully, knowing that she was terrified of what it might be.

'Because you were my friend,' I said at last. 'Back when you were only little, you were my friend, and I probably got a lot more out of that friendship than you did.'

'How?'

'I was only a student when I worked with you before. I was learning how to be a childcare worker. You taught me an awful lot just by letting me be around you. I left, and I don't think I even said goodbye.'

'I don't remember.'

'Neither do I, which makes me think I didn't. I was young, only a teenager, and I was probably afraid of making a dork of *myself* if I said goodbye to you.'

'Really?'

'Yep.'

'I don't think I would have minded.'

'I know that now. I guess there was a bit more for me to learn.'

'It's nice you liked me enough to be worried about that.'

'I did. I still do. I wouldn't be here if I didn't.'

'I know. Thanks.'

And I half knelt/half crouched there, with her clinging to me for dear life and my legs going numb as night bore down on us and the city honked and hissed and blared beyond the window.

12

I went to see Mr and Mrs Byrne two days later.

They had been moved from the near-derelict structure they owned, where they had systematically tortured
Larry and Francey, and placed in a small local authority
house close to the city centre. I took a bus to the secluded
estate and arrived shortly after ten in the morning. Loud
country and western music was blaring through the front
door, and I had to knock hard before I finally gained
admittance.

Vera Byrne was probably not five feet in platforms.
She had long, dishwater-blonde hair and prominent buck-
teeth. Her eyebrows formed one single line of dense hair
across her forehead, and she had a pronounced squint.
There was about her a steely intelligence, though.

Malachi Byrne, on the other hand, was over six feet
tall with a pendulous gut and an upper body so wide he
had to turn sideways to get through most doorways. This
great bulk sat atop two skinny, short legs, making him
look like he was on the verge of overbalancing all the
time. He had little hair, and what he did have was cropped
close to his skull in a crew cut. His face, which was
swathed in great rolls of fatty flesh, contained two small,
round eyes that were set close together and gave him a
slow-witted, indolent look.

'Turn down the tape, Mal,' Vera roared over the noise as she showed me into the kitchen. 'We've a visitor.'

The house was sparsely furnished and decorated. There were no pictures on the walls and no ornaments or oddments anywhere. I sat on a narrow couch and waited while they busied themselves making tea and laying some crumbly digestive biscuits on a plate.

'I'm not staying long,' I said, as the pair pulled over straight-backed kitchen chairs and eyed me with open suspicion. 'I just want to ask a favour, really.'

'Go on, speak your mind,' Vera said, smiling in a way that was making me feel decidedly uncomfortable. It was how I imagined a fox would view a rabbit just before it sprang.

'I was wondering if you could give me a loan of the keys to your place in Oldtown.'

'Now why would you be wantin' those?' Vera asked, continuing to leer. She had a habit of breathing through her mouth rather than her nose, and the sound of her sucking air in and out over those incisors was horrible. Her breath was rank too. I could smell it from where I sat.

'I want to bring Larry and Francey back there for a visit. I think it would be good for them.'

'You're up to something,' Vera said, her smile broadening. 'Have a bicky.'

'Thank you, no.'

'So why do you really want to go back to our home? Why should I give you the keys to the kingdom?'

'Your children are trying to make some sense of what has happened to them, Mrs Byrne. I believe that returning to the place where they grew up would be beneficial. They might be better able to put things in context.'

She looked at her husband, smacking her thin lips and shaking her head in a mock of confusion. 'He sure talks sweet, doesn't he, Mal? What do you think he meant by all that palaver?'

'I don't know, Vera.' The big man's voice was deep and stentorian. He seemed to speak only when spoken to, and spent most his time in still silence.

'What are you actually sayin', young fella?' Vera hissed.

'That your children need to get back into the house where it seems some frightening things happened to them. You would be doing them a great service, and showing yourselves willing to help with their recovery, by giving me the keys.'

She leaned close, her brow almost touching mine. I held my breath against the reek of her.

'Tell me now, young man. What do you think happened to them?'

'It doesn't matter what I think, Mrs Byrne,' I said through gritted teeth, trying hard not to retch. 'It's what I *know* that counts.'

'And what do you know?'

I thought about laying my cards on the table. It would have been good to freak the harridan out by telling her exactly what I knew of her. But I held back. I realized that there was much I still did not know. The children had given us only hints, allusions, hazy phantoms of what they had experienced. The way to break through the barrier of fear and suppression was to bring them back, and to do that I needed their parents' permission. My great fear was that the twins weren't ready, that making them relive their experiences would be too much. I did not want to shatter the tenuous equilibrium they had achieved.

'I don't know anything, Mrs Byrne. The children have said very little.'

'Humph,' she grunted and sat back.

I shuddered, not caring if they saw it or not. 'Can I have the keys, then?'

'Give them to him, Mal,' she snapped.

The huge man stood up and stomped from the room.

'When do I get my children back?' she hissed at me when we were alone. 'They belong to me, and I want them.'

'I have no say over that. It's up to the courts.'

'You tell them I want my children back, and I shall have them, come hell or high water. You can't keep me from what's mine.'

'It's not as simple as that, Mrs Byrne.'

'Oh, it is.' She raised her hand to shush me, displaying long, cracked fingernails. 'It *is* that simple. Give them to me, or I'll come and take them. I don't care which way it goes. Either is just grand with me.'

'Do you realize what you're saying, Mrs Byrne? You have just told me you intend to abduct your children unless they are returned to you.'

She suddenly burst into a gurgling, throaty cackle, tossing her head back and slapping her bony knees, spraying me with foul saliva in the process.

'Oh Christ, d'you hear him? Now I may well have said

that, but there's nobody here but you and me, and I don't recall sayin' anythin' of the sort.'

'I just heard you.'

She leaned in close again, and this time I pulled back from her proximity.

'Well, isn't it an awful pity you didn't have a tape recorder with you?'

Malachi Byrne lumbered back in with a huge bundle of rusted keys on a metal loop. He tossed it at me, and they hit the back of the couch where I sat with a heavy thud.

'Go on,' she said. 'Play your games. Get those keys back to us by next week, no later. That's still our house, and we'll be returning there one of these days. I'll be having those two little ones back soon enough, too, so make the best of them while you can. Show him the door, Mal, my love.'

A hand like a shovel made to grab me by the shoulder, but I twisted away and shot out of his reach.

'I can find my way, thank you.'

My phone rang as I walked back to the bus stop. I looked at the display, but the number had been withheld.

'Yes?'

'It's Devereux. I think I may have something.'

'Go on.' Mina had been missing for three days, now, and the chances of finding her were getting slimmer by the hour.

'I have the name of someone with the particular ... propensities we discussed. He fits the description of the man you encountered in The Sailing Cot.'

'Do you have an address?'

'Not yet. But I will. Probably by this evening. We should move as soon as possible.'

'Agreed. Call me.'

'We'll talk later.'

Olwyn seemed to have abandoned the Goth look completely. She was not due on shift that morning, and I met her at an Internet café near where she lived. She told me airily that she was a huge fan of *Buffy the Vampire Slayer*, and had developed several websites which she spent nearly all her free time maintaining. But the coffee was very good and the geek factor was always entertaining, so I didn't complain.

'Why *Buffy*?' I asked out of idle curiosity as she tapped away at the keyboard, her eyes glued to the monitor.

'Because it's the best thing on TV. And it speaks to me. I see a lot of my life in there.'

'Ah, but is it better than *The Simpsons*?'

'Different types of shows. I don't really watch cartoons.'

'Do you watch anything other than *Buffy* and *Angel*?'

'Um . . . no.'

'Hard to make any comparisons, then.'

'S'pose.'

I watched her continue to post whatever comment she was broadcasting across the globe via the world-wide-web. A skinny kid sitting on the other side of me puffed on an asthma inhaler. Two pre-pubescents across the room were arguing the relative merits of Peter Jackson's *Lord of the Rings* versus Ralph Bakshi's cartoon version. The fact that I actually knew what they were talking about made me wonder about my own nerd credentials, which caused me to feel a bit uncomfortable, so I stopped listening. Finally, Olwyn swung her chair away from the screen and smiled at me. 'So, what's up?'

I hoisted the keys up onto the desk in front of her. She stared at them.

'What are those?'

'The keys to the Byrne homestead.'

'Why are you showing them to me?'

'I want to bring Larry and Francey back there.'

She turned pale. Without the make-up she was actually quite a pretty girl. My heart went out to her. She knew what I was about to ask, and I watched her struggle with the desire to tell me to go to hell.

'Why are you telling me this?'

'I want you to come with me.'

'But . . . but I'm a screw-up. I'm no good, Shane. Take someone else.'

'Who?'

'Karena. Bríd, maybe.'

'There's no bond there. The twins haven't shown any affection or interest in anyone else. You're the only person on the staff team either of the twins has formed an attachment to. Which makes you the obvious choice.'

She was still gazing at the keys. I had to admit, they were quite a sight; these were not the modern type, but the big, ornate pieces of ironmongery from the doors of an old home with ancient, heavy locks. There was a weighty symbolism at play. I was aware of it – how could I fail to be? Here were the keys to these tormented children's souls. We were about to open Pandora's Box.

'I . . . I don't want to go. I'm sorry. I just can't.'

'Why?'

'I'm afraid of what we'll find.'

'Me too.'

She reached over to touch the keys and pulled back, as if they were conducting an electric charge.

'Do you really think going out there will do any good?' she asked, looking at me at last.

'I don't know. I hope that the children will take us on a kind of tour, tell us what their lives were like when they lived there. I'm going to ask them to show us where they slept and ate and played, and we'll just have to see what comes out. I imagine it'll be fairly unpleasant stuff, and that they'll maybe freak out a little. But the precise details . . . we'll just have to wait and see.'

'But you must have some idea.'

'Yes, but only suspicions. I think that it's going to be a difficult, horrible experience for all four of us. But I firmly believe – no, strike that – I *know* that it's the only way we're ever going to get through to the twins. I can't do it on my own, and I need someone with me they'll respond to if it gets rough, which it probably will.'

'When do you want to go?'

'This afternoon.'

'Oh God!'

She buried her face in her hands. I knew how she was feeling, because I was feeling it too. I didn't want to do this any more than she did. But there was no other way.

She spoke through her fingers, as if confining herself to darkness would make it somehow easier.

'All right.'

'Thank you.'

'Tell me it'll be okay. That we'll be fine and they'll be better afterwards.'

'I can't. But whatever comes, we'll deal with it as best we can.'

'I don't think I really want to know what happened to them. I think I'm better off not knowing.'

I looked about us at the acned, greasy-haired, bespectacled young people, engrossed in their sci-fi and role-playing games and cult television shows.

'It's part of our job, unfortunately, to know things that other people don't,' I said. 'It's the toughest part of what we do, without a doubt. You're right, you probably *are* better off not knowing. You could live the rest of your life in perfect happiness without ever giving it another moment's thought. By going with me this afternoon, you'll see things and hear things that will stay with you and haunt your dreams and maybe a little bit of you will remain in the old house with whatever we find there. I'm not going to lie to you about that. But by doing it, we're giving Larry and Francey a chance to heal. With a bit of luck, they'll come out the other side happier and more at peace, because we'll have helped them to exorcize whatever demons are inside them. And that's what makes it worthwhile. That's how you do it, see? By remembering *why* you do it.'

She sighed deeply and spun back around to the computer and its glowing screen.

'I'll be at work this afternoon,' she said. 'I need to finish this now.'

I nodded and stood up, taking the heavy bundle of keys with me.

'I'll see you later.'

She didn't look at me or respond. She was back where she was happiest, in a place where the monsters weren't real.

The Byrne house nestled like a tumour into the hustle and bustle of Oldtown. It had been there before the ghetto had developed, a remnant from another time, somehow still clinging to its otherness. An ugly wreckage, it was a three-storey townhouse, surrounded by walls on three sides and with iron railings out front. An overgrown field of maybe half an acre backed onto the property – had probably belonged to it at some point in the past. I wondered who owned it now. It made no sense that no one had built apartments or an office block on it. But then, who would want to live or set up a business next door to this nightmarish house? It exuded a palpable atmosphere of being somehow off-kilter. I was reminded of the house of cake in *Hansel and Gretel*. This structure was just as strange and out of place.

Larry and Francey sat in the back seat of the Austin, craning their necks like meerkats to see out of the windows, looks of strange excitement on their faces. They seemed eager to be off; there was no trace of the worry or anxiety I had expected. I had gone straight to Rivendell after meeting Olwyn, and told the children of my plans. I was worried about their reaction and wanted them to have time to prepare themselves. But they shrugged off the news, apparently unconcerned.

'Why d'you want to go to that ol' place?' Larry demanded. 'There don' be nu'in there no more. Mammy and Daddy is goned.'

He had got over the fright he'd experienced during the storytelling, but had retreated back into the 'everything is fine and I'll be going home soon' fantasy. It was as if his veiled disclosures had never happened.

'I want you to show me where you lived,' I said. 'Me and Olwyn.'

'Whatchoo bringin' *her* 'long for?' Francey asked. 'She bes a fierce dumb girl. We don' need her 'tall.'

'I've asked her to come. I can't take you in the car on my own; it's not allowed. Anyway, it's not nice to call someone dumb, especially someone who has only ever tried to be nice to you.'

'Let 'er come, Francey,' Larry said.

'She messded you up, Lar,' Francey said guardedly. 'You did go all funny on me, an' it was cause o' her.'

'No 'twasn't,' Larry countered. 'I was messded up 'fore she comed along. She's alrigh'.'

'But –'

'But nu'in. I don' wanna talk 'bou' it no more. She bes a nice 'nough person an' I don' mind 'er comin'.'

Francey gave him a poisonous look and sulked for the rest of the morning, but when Olwyn arrived, and had finished the usual handover meeting with the staff coming off the previous shift, we all got into the car and made for Oldtown, and the bad moods were forgotten.

I parked outside the railings, which had been painted black sometime in the past twenty years, but were now rusted and peeling. The front gate was chained and padlocked, and I sorted through the huge bunch of keys and found the right one. The gate creaked open. No one moved for a second, then with a whoop the twins bolted past Olwyn and me and disappeared around the side of the main building.

'I don't like the feel of this. The vibes are really bad,' Olwyn said, gripping my arm tightly.

'We'll be lucky if bad vibes are the worst things we'll have to deal with,' I said. 'Come on.'

There was a small patch of dirt in front of the house, which had probably been intended as a lawn but had never been properly seeded, now dotted here and there with weeds and some foul-looking fungi. A path, cracked and subsided, ran across it.

The rear of the property consisted of a large yard, covered in concrete with reeds and scutch grass poking through the cracks. A wooden shed with a roof of corrugated iron sat off to one side. A section of the rear wall had been knocked through to allow access to the adjoining field. The house appeared to have a basement, because steps led below ground level in two flights, one to the back door of the house and then down from that again to another door. There was no sign of the children, but cries and shrieks told us that they had gone right through the yard and into the field.

They were up an old tree in the west corner, laughing and calling to one another. Olwyn and I approached slowly. They knew we were there, but ignored us. They seemed to be in a state of heightened excitement now, teetering on the brink of losing control, the stimuli of being back home almost too much for them. Language had been abandoned, giving way to animal cries and gestures.

I let them play for ten minutes or so, as they acclimatized themselves to their old stomping ground, then jangled the keys loudly.

'So where'll we go first? The house? The shed?'

That silenced them, and they sat on their perches, eyeing us solemnly. Then in a clatter of rapid movement they were back on the ground.

'Le's go to the house,' Francey said. 'C'mon. I'll show ya.'

I wanted to go and see the shed, which I believed would bring back the most vivid memories, but I was conscious of this being their home, and that we were there as guests. They would show us at their own pace. The exercise was about their needs, not mine.

They led us down the narrow steps to the back door. A damp, thin coating of moss made the going treacherous. Moisture seemed to have caused the frame to swell, and the door stuck at first, but then gave and stiffly opened. A blast of foul air assailed us. Larry and Francey, seeming not to notice, shoved their way inside and were off again into the bowels of the building. We followed less enthusiastically.

The Byrnes' old home was as cluttered and gaudily bedecked as their new one was spartan. Every wall creaked with paintings and ornaments, each mantelpiece and shelf loaded down with clutter. Nothing matched, not a single item complemented those about it. It was like whoever had chosen them had purposefully set out to construct a look that set the nerves on edge and offended the eye.

'Oh – my – God,' Olwyn said, her eyes wide. 'This is fucking insane.'

'Why'd they leave all their stuff?' I asked. 'Their new place looks as if they barely own the clothes on their back. They've just abandoned everything.'

'Maybe they're not planning on staying away for very long,' Olwyn said.

'Vera, the mother, told me that she wouldn't be kept from what was hers. Maybe she meant this place, too. She *did* say they'd be coming back eventually.'

'Why'd they leave, then?'

'They claim to want the children back. The Health Executive told them the building wasn't fit for human habitation, and if there was to be any chance of reunification, they'd have to move somewhere safe. I think the Byrnes are playing a game with us: follow the rules and then, when the family's together again, go back to things as they were.'

'Could they be that calculating?'

'Mrs Byrne certainly could.'

The house had been empty for only a couple of months, but there was dust and filth that spoke of years of neglect. The floor of the kitchen we stood in was covered in grease and grime. Crumbs and scraps of mould encrusted a heavy wooden table by the window; a chair blanketed in spiders' webs huddled against the wall. We walked through the kitchen area into a hallway that ran the length of the house. The floorboards, once burnished oak, were now frosted with dust and grooved with deep scratches and scuffs. A grotesque animal head hung over the front door. I couldn't tell what creature it had originally been – the taxidermist was a talentless amateur. The skin hung in furry flaps, and bone showed through in pale patches. I pulled my gaze away from it and turned to the staircase. It was a beautiful piece of work, seemingly carved from a single piece of wood. It curved around majestically, travelling up through the levels of the house. A trapdoor at my feet told me that it also went down through the boards to the basement levels below. Placing my hand on the banisters, I realized this was the spine of the building.

Looking upwards, I saw Francey standing stock-still above us on the first landing. She looked very pale, but a sheen of sweat glistened on her forehead. The house had already left its mark on her – scum and filth were ingrained into her once clean clothes and a scratch, possibly from the branches of the tree, ran across her cheek.

'Come up,' she said, and then was gone from view.

We followed their voices along the corridor to a room overlooking the street. In it were two children's beds and nothing else. The plaster on the wall was cracked and the boards were bare and unvarnished. There were no toys, no books, no sign that anyone had ever done anything but slept here. It was a dead, empty room. Everywhere else in the house vibrated with the foreboding personality of those who had gone before: generations of Byrnes. But not this sad little alcove.

Larry sat among the dusty blankets on one of the beds. Francey stood by the door, watching him.

'This was our room, so it was,' she said when we came in.

'It's . . . lovely,' Olwyn said, and I cringed inwardly. The children were not stupid. The room was anything but lovely, and they knew it.

'They said it was our room,' Larry intoned gently, as if he was talking to himself. 'But we never slept here. Not hardly ever, anyway. I don' 'member sleepin' here. Do you, Francey?'

'No,' she said.

'Where did you sleep, then?' I asked. 'Can you show me?'

They said nothing for a while. Larry was gently rocking, the filthy bed linen wrapped around his shoulders. Francey seemed in a kind of trance, her hair lank, covered in dust-devils. Finally Larry stirred and seemed to see us for the first time.

'Sometimes,' he said, 'they'd put us down to bed here. Not much, but sometimes. We knowed, though, that she'd come for us 'fore too long.'

Francey laughed, but it was an uncomfortable sound.

'She used say: "Get up, lazybones",' Francey giggled. '"Get up, lazybones. I wants my fun."'

'And we'd have t' go t' their room wit the big bed.'

Francey laughed and, turning on her heel, skipped through the door. I followed her onto the landing, and when I got there she was dancing up the next flight of stairs.

'Come on, I'll show you,' she said happily. Larry walked past me slowly, as if some irrefutable force was drawing him. 'You had to go when she told ya,' he said as he went towards the stairs. 'You'd be whipped anyway, but it was worse if you di'n't go when she said.'

The master bedroom was right at the end of the top floor. I could hear Francey singing inside: *Jack and Jill went up the hill to fetch a pail of water*. She was using a strange, sing-song melody, her voice rising and falling lightly, until she got to the line: *Jack fell down and broke his crown*, which she shouted with all her might.

The room was dominated by a four-poster bed of enormous size, complete with drapes. Francey sat in the centre of it, singing. Larry was on the floor, his knees up at his chin, rocking again.

'This bes where we'd be took,' she said matter-of-factly. 'This bes where Mammy slept wit Daddy in this here bed.'

'Why did they take you here?' Olwyn asked, her voice shaking.

Francey smiled, a glint in her eye. She knew the discomfort this was causing both of us, but was relishing Olwyn's inability to hide it.

'She liked Lar to do tings to her sometimes. Or she made Daddy have sex on me. And she had me and Lar do stuff to each other now 'n' again. Other times, she'd lock us up in that.' She pointed at a door set into the wall.

I tried the handle, but it was locked. Again I fumbled through the heavy set of keys, and finally one fitted and turned. Inside was a cupboard. The shelves and poles had been removed to create a small space, and the wooden interior was covered with what looked like the scratches of fingernails. A substance was encrusted onto the floor and the lower parts of the walls. I could guess what it was, but didn't ask for confirmation. There was just about enough space for the two children in there, but with barely any room to move inside. It was like a coffin.

'How long did they keep you in there for?'

'Not long, like when they put us in the shed,' Francey said. 'But 'twas always dark inside, so 'twas hard to tell if 'twas daytime or nigh'time. We'd only get lockded up in there if we was really bad. Once, they pu' Lar in there by hisself. He screamed and screamed and banged and I thinked he was goin't' break the door off.'

'I din' like 't in there on my own,' Larry said. 'I was fierce scairt. Mammy dragged me out and she took a belt to me till my back was all cutted, then she put me back in.'

'You din' scream that time,' Francey grinned. She stood up and bounced off the bed in two leaps. 'Come on, I wants to show you our shed.'

I was never so glad to feel fresh air on my face. Olwyn looked as if she were on the verge of being sick. I took her hand and squeezed it. She smiled sheepishly and squeezed back.

The door of the shed swung open without any need for keys: the police had broken it open when the children had been seized and taken into care, and it had never been fixed. Inside I could see it had been a commonly used dwelling place over many years. The floor, which was bare dirt, was worn smooth with use, and clumps of desiccated faeces lay here and there. Despite the door being partially open there was still a powerful smell of urine in the air.

'Sometimes, when we knowed they was asleep, we used

get ou' this away,' Larry said, pushing aside a loose board.

'To play with the cat?' I asked.

'You told him 'bou' the cat?' Francey snarled, colour rising in her cheeks. 'We said we wouldn't *never* —'

'I only said we used play wit 'im,' Larry said as she bore down on him. 'I din' tell th' udder stuff.'

The little girl was suddenly furious. She had treated the whole visit like a game up until then. Even her mention of sexual abuse had been in an airy and frivolous tone. But now she was angry, and terribly so.

'We said we'd never, ever talk 'bou' tha' again, Lar! You promised me! Why'd you tell?'

'I din' tell, really I din',' Larry said, tears streaming down his face now at his twin's rage.

'Francey,' I said, completely surprised at her response, 'all Larry said was that there was a nice cat who would come and sit at the window of the shed, and that you would watch him catch birds and play with him. If there's more to the story, I never heard it.'

She turned on me, a fury that was raw and visceral in her eyes. There were no tears. She was beyond them.

'You shouldna' bringed us back here,' she screamed at me. 'You had no righ' to bring us to this here place!' With that she kicked the loose board aside and sprang out through the opening.

Through the yellow filth of the window I saw her leap over the wall and vanish into the field. Olwyn was holding Larry, who was sobbing inconsolably.

'I'm sorry, Larry,' I said to him, squatting down beside them. 'You never said not to talk about the cat. I didn't mean to make her mad like that.'

He didn't answer, just buried his face in Olwyn's shoulder.

'Go and get her,' Olwyn said through her own tears. 'She can't have gone far.'

I left them.

Francey was in the tree they'd been in earlier. I stood at the base and gazed up at her. She hadn't climbed very high, just a little above my head. She watched me approach, and I saw that the rage had mostly burned out already.

'You leave me 'lone,' she said sulkily. 'I don't wanna talk 'bou' it.'

'I'm sorry I upset you, Francey. I don't know what I said that made you so mad, but whatever it was, I apologize. I'd like you, when you're feeling a bit better, to say sorry to Larry too. He's really sad, and I know you don't like it when he's unhappy.'

'He shouldn't telled you 'bou' tha' cat! It was our secret and he telled!'

'What's so terrible about playing with a cat?'

'*I'll tell you what's so awful! They found out and they killded it!*'

She screamed the words at me, the ejaculation followed by a string of shrieks that left her hoarse. I waited until she'd finished, then climbed up beside her. As an adult, I always feel stupid up trees, and this time was no different. I sat a little away and said nothing. She was crying softly now, beating her fist gently off the branch. Finally she said: 'We used love tha' cat. We din' have no friends, but we had him. He likeded us an' ev'ry time we was in tha' shed he'd come and keep us comp'ny. He teached us to feed ourselves.'

'Larry told me. That was pretty smart of you.'

'It nearly wasn' so bad bein' left ou'side when he was wit us. We was like a li'l fambly of our own. Sometimes we'd let 'im in t'rough the board and snuggle up t' him at nigh', an' he'd be rale warm. Tha's how she found ou' 'bout 'im.'

'Are you sure you want to talk about it, Francey? It's been a tough afternoon for you.'

She nodded, tears running in a steady flow, but her voice firm now.

'We'd letted 'im in one nigh' when it was rale cold. We was never gived no blankets or anyt'in', so we bringed him in for the heat and went t' sleep. I wakeded up and she was standin' there, lookin' down at us, an' she had 'im. He was a big ol' cat, but he just hanged there from her hand, like he knowed he was gonna die and there wasn' nu'in he could do 'bou' it. He prob'ly could've fighted her, but he din'.'

'Cat's are funny sometimes. You just don't know what they'll do.'

'She kicked Lar till he wakeded up, then she tole us to folla her, an' she went into th' kitchen. She tooked a knife.'

She choked then, and couldn't continue for a time.

Finally: 'She tole Daddy to hold the cat, an' she tooked the knife, and she sticked it into his belly, and she cut him so's all his guts comed out. He made a awful noise when she done it, then he din' make noise no more.'

'That must have been terrible for you to see,' I said, scarcely able to imagine the horror they must have felt. 'It was a very cruel thing to do.'

'She made us watch while Daddy pulled all the skin off of our cat, an' then she tooked the chopper, and she . . . she cutted off his legs and his head an' cut his body up into li'l bits.'

I knew what was coming, but I hoped I was wrong.

'Then she put on a big burner, an' she filled it up wit water an' she cutted up vegetables an' she put all the bits of him in there. "You is always sayin' how you is *sooo* hungry," she says. "Well here bes a special dinner, and I wants you to eat it all up."'

Francey sighed a deep sigh.

'We eated it, alrigh'. We was always hungry, an' he would've wanted us to. I tried to on'y eat the vegetables, but she kep' hittin' me 'till I eated the bits of him, too.'

It was mid-afternoon. The sun shone down on us from a sky dotted with clouds. Swallows darted here and there, chasing insects. In a neighbouring tree a blackbird sang its beautiful warbling song. And, in the midst of this idyllic summer's day, was a child trapped in a nightmare of unwavering evil and sadism from which she could not awake.

13

It was dark when the call came from Devereux. He asked me to meet him outside The Sailing Cot, and half an hour later I was standing with him below the swinging sign. I was almost hopping from foot to foot in my desire to get going, but he was calm and immutable, as always.

'The man's name is Terence Fields. I have been informed that those who wish to contact him come here. I was unsuccessful in ascertaining his home address by my usual means.'

'Shit,' I said, kicking the kerb in frustration. 'They don't like me in there. There's no way they'll tell us anything.'

Devereux allowed himself a smile. 'They may tell me.'

I shrugged. 'Well, it can't hurt to try. Let's go.'

The pub was busier than I had ever seen it, the crowd at the bar several people deep. The landlord was serving, along with one of the 'bouncers' he had called for that first evening I had been there and found Fields with Mina. Devereux moved through the throng like Moses parting the Red Sea. People just seemed to naturally move out of his way. When we got to the front, he called to the proprietor: 'Mr Murphy, I require some information.'

The older man glanced at him, then at me, and whispered something to his large compatriot. The bouncer lumbered over and leant in close to Devereux. 'The management would like yiz to leave. Now get out of here before there's trouble.'

I was standing right next to Devereux, and never saw him move. But he must have done something, because one moment the thug behind the bar was leaning in to him, trying to look threatening, the next he was sprawled against the taps, trying to staunch the flow of blood from his nose. It happened so quickly and quietly that the crowd around us didn't even notice, the bleeding man receiving a few funny looks.

'Jesus, Johnny, you'd want to get that looked at,' someone said to him.

Devereux reached over and grabbed the bigger man. He weighed probably twenty kilos less, and was nearly half a metre shorter, but this difference in size seemed not to faze him one iota. It looked as if he was patting the bruiser on the shoulder, but I could see he was not. He pulled him up so that he could speak quietly into his ear. 'I wish to find Terence Fields. He has something I need returned. Now, you and your employer should know that I can cause a good deal of upset, and I will keep coming back here until I receive the correct information. So, why don't you go and tend to that nosebleed, and while you're on your way to the Gents, tell your boss to write the correct address on the back of a beer-mat and pass it over to my friend here?'

Holding his nose in a cupped hand, the injured bouncer whispered something to the landlord, then went out the back. The older man cast us a filthy look, but took a biro from his breast pocket and wrote something on a scrap of paper. He thrust it across the bar at me.

'Take it and get the fuck out of my pub,' he hissed at me. 'Take your pal and don't come back.'

'Thank you,' Devereux smiled. 'Let's hope we don't need to.'

The address given was for a tenement flat on the waterfront, not far from where we were. As we walked, Devereux cast regular glances back over his shoulder to ensure that we weren't being followed. He needn't have worried.

The front door was ajar, and we climbed four flights of stairs until we were standing outside the correct number. I could hear *Dire Straits* playing quietly inside. I raised my hand to knock, but Devereux caught it.

'We don't know what we'll encounter behind that door,' he said. 'She may be in there, she may not. We have no idea what condition she'll be in if she is inside. We lack any knowledge of how many men we'll find, or if they'll offer any resistance to us taking her. If it goes bad, grab her if you can, and get out. Don't concern yourself with me.'

I nodded, my heart pounding, sweat soaking the back of my T-shirt. He grasped my arm and winked.

'It'll be fine. Just stay behind me until we see what the story is, then do what you have to. Ready?'

I nodded again. He rapped loudly on the door. At first all we could hear was Mark Knopfler regaling us with tales of private investigations. Then shuffling footsteps.

'Who is it?'

'Gardaí.' Devereux's voice was usually unaccented, but now he spoke with thick West of Ireland inflections. He sounded just like a big, country guard. 'We had a complaint about noise. Could I have a few words with the man of the house?'

A key rattled in a lock. Devereux stepped back, balancing on the balls of his feet, and as soon as the door opened a crack, he planted a kick right below the handle. The door crashed in, knocking the person behind it aside, and Devereux slipped through, followed by me. *Two counts of assault. One count of impersonating a police officer, one count of forced entry*, I thought. *Even by my standards, this is a bad night.*

A short hallway led to the main living area. I was immediately aware of the smell of marijuana, but there was cigarette smoke and alcohol also.

'Hey,' the man Devereux had knocked aside shouted, 'ye can't just barge in like this. I know my rights.'

'Shut up,' Devereux said, and the tone of his voice quelled the man immediately.

There were six of them in the living area, sprawled on two long couches and a couple of armchairs. They were all middle aged, most of them in their underwear, all obviously drunk, stoned or both. Cans of cheap lager littered the floor, two hash-pipes and an ashtray full of butts were on the table. Lying across the lap of one of the men, wearing an open shirt and nothing else, was Mina. I spotted Fields among the group. He recognized me, as I did him, and he began to sit up.

'Stay where you are,' Devereux said quietly, and Fields stopped moving. I went to Mina. The man she was draped over was so out of it, he barely noticed me. She seemed to be asleep, and I shook her gently. Slowly, her eyes opened and she saw me.

'Mina, I'm taking you home,' I said. 'Come on, love. It's okay.'

Tears came to her eyes, and she nodded, reaching out to me. I looked about the mess on the floor and found a jacket, which I wrapped around her, and got her standing up. As she moved across the room, I noticed she was limping.

'What did you do to her?' I asked, realizing that I was crying too, but not caring.

'Nothin' she didn't want done,' Fields said, starting to roll a joint. 'Take 'er. We're done with 'er anyway.'

Anger came over me in a great wave. Mina was leaning on me, breathing hard with the exertion of simply standing. I looked back at the vermin sitting among the detritus of their tenement room. If I'd had a can of petrol, I would gladly have torched the place.

'Shane, we have the girl. There's nothing left for us here.' Devereux steered me towards the door. 'There will be other days to follow up on what we've just seen. The child needs a hospital.'

We got her to the Austin and I lay her on the back seat. She was shivering now, and I was worried that shock had set in. I turned to Devereux. 'Thank you, Karl. I couldn't have done that without you.'

He nodded, patted me on the shoulder, and strolled away into the night. On my way to the hospital, I added *breaking the speed limit and running five red lights* to the list.

Ben Tyrrell shook me awake at six thirty the following morning. I had fallen asleep in a chair in the corridor outside Mina's room. They had made her comfortable, given her something to help her sleep, and she was to see a doctor later that day. Her parents were in with her. I knew they'd have questions, and had stayed around, but it seemed that fear of the answers that would follow had, as yet, prevented them coming out to me.

'How about that cup of coffee I owe you?' Ben asked.

'Throw in some breakfast and you've got a deal.'

'Come on. The canteen here needs to be shut down for health reasons. There's a good place across the road, though.'

'You're on. Just let me tell Dirk and Molly, and I'll be with you.'

I knocked and stuck my head round the door. Molly was asleep on a camp-bed next to her daughter. Dirk was standing with his back to them, staring out the window.

'I'm popping out for half an hour, Dirk. I'll be back, though.'

His back remained to me.

'Of course, Shane. I'm sorry, I forgot you were still here. I'll talk to you later.'

'Okay, then.'

We got a table among the medical staff who were the diner's main trade.

'So, tell me what happened,' Ben said.

I did.

He asked no questions and made no comment until I had finished.

'You found her. Well done. I don't think there's anyone else on the team, myself included, who could have done it.'

'I didn't find her. Devereux did.'

'True. And that was a . . . creative approach, calling him in.'

'You don't approve?'

'You've been doing this work long enough to know that there is very little black and white. Most of what we do is a sea of sludgy grey. I think Devereux is on the side of the angels now. If you'd asked my advice, I probably wouldn't have recommended him, but I'm glad you sought him out. It got the job done.'

'What are we going to do with the Henrys? They've been to hell and back. I only gave them a cursory picture of what happened, but I reckon they've been able to fill in the blanks themselves.'

'They can afford private counselling. I'll put them in touch with someone good.'

'They need more than counselling. I think some long-term family support may be necessary.'

'I agree. But I believe they're out of the woods. It's a great pity it had to come to this, but you did as much as you could to prevent it.'

'I pray to God she's okay. Those bastards took turns on her. Goddammit, they had her for days . . .'

I felt tears returning and squeezed my eyes shut, willing them away.

'They won't walk away from this unscathed,' Ben said. 'I know Devereux, and you will probably find that they'll all pay a price in one way or another.'

I nodded, rubbing my eyes with the heels of my hands.

'Ben, I need a favour.'

'Certainly. If I can help, I will.'

'It's personal.'

'Shoot.'

I told him about Sylvie. He listened gravely.

'You should have come to me with this a long time ago, Shane.'

'I know.'

'You put yourself and the child at risk.'

'Can you help her?'

He relit the butt of his cigarette. 'The father hasn't returned?'

'No. She doesn't think he will. I've given her a mobile phone and enough credit to do her for a while. My number is set on speed-dial, so even if he does come back, all she has to do is hit the number one, and I'll know she's in trouble. I believe he's gone to ground, though.'

'We can't depend on that.'

'Is there somewhere she can go where she'll be able to keep the child? I don't think she'll survive if they take the baby away from her.'

'I'll see what I can do. You went rogue on this one, Shane. It's a tendency you have, and I don't like it. This is a team sport, and we cannot afford to have any soloists. In future, you come to me and we sort it out together. Are we clear?'

'Yes. I'm sorry, Ben.'

He looked me directly in the eye. 'You lost one, during your last job, didn't you?'

'Yes.'

'Gillian, wasn't it?'

'Yes.'

'You thought if you could save Sylvie, all by yourself, it might cancel that failure.'

The tears came and I couldn't stop them this time. I was tired and sick and my head ached with the pain and sorrow that was all about me. I hadn't asked for this. I had tried to avoid it, in fact. How the fuck had I ended up back here? I thought that I'd run far, far away from all the mixed emotions and confusion. Somehow, they had caught up with me again.

'I don't know. Probably.'

'We'll save Sylvie. It sounds like you already have, pretty much.'

'She got beaten to within an inch of her life.'

'But he's gone. Grey areas, Shane. There are often trade-offs. That was one of them. You made a judgement call. In the back of your mind, you knew when you confronted him that there was a possibility he'd take it out on her. He did, but, in the long term, it has paid off. He's gone, and we can now *really* help these two children.'

'I'm tired, Ben. I don't know if I can keep this up much longer.'

'Go home. I'll stay with the Henrys. Get a few hours' sleep in a bed. Have a shower. You and I have a meeting at three this afternoon with a psychologist, regarding Bobby and Micky Walsh.'

'Excellent. That's positive.'

'I hope so. I tend to be a bit dubious about shrinks, but I think it's a step in the right direction. But then, I've been waiting for three months for this chap to return my call, so anything's better than that.'

I stood up.

'I'm going home. Call me if there's any news about Mina. I'll see you at Last Ditch House later.'

'That would be good.'

I got to the office a little early. Ben and the psychologist were in the meeting room, and I took a seat at the table with them. I was feeling much better after five hours' sleep and a pot of coffee. Now, with this man ready to help us with Bobby and Micky, it seemed things were taking a turn for the better. Ben introduced us.

'Shane, this is Dr James Kilshannon, Head Psychologist with Child and Adolescent Psychiatry for the City Health Executive.'

The good doctor was maybe thirty, with a nice haircut, clean-shaven, wearing sensible yet fashionable square-lensed glasses and a neatly tailored grey summer suit with a wine-coloured tie. Ben and I looked like a pair of out-and-out hippies beside him. Which, in fairness, we were.

'Doctor, thanks for coming,' I said, shaking his hand. 'I can't tell you how relieved I am. I'll be honest: I'm starting to feel more than a little out of my depth on this case.'

I passed the file over, and he spent ten minutes poring over the reports, pictures and various other pieces of evidence I had accumulated over the month and a half I'd spent working with the boys.

'This is really fascinating.'

'Any thoughts?' Ben asked.

'Simultaneous group hysteria, perhaps. I've read

reports of abnormal psychic transference between close siblings. I've never encountered it in practice, but it's not unheard of. Some kind of collective unconscious communication? It could be any of those three things. Really fascinating. There's definitely the makings of a research paper here, that's for sure. Neither of you are writing one, are you?'

'Not just at present, no,' Ben smiled.

'Good, good.'

'When can you start, doctor?'

He blinked at us behind his lenses. 'Well, there's a waiting list of around a year in our department just at the moment. Cutbacks, you see.'

'But in this instance, an exception will be made,' Ben said firmly.

'Oh, certainly. We'll speed things along.'

'I knew you would,' Ben grinned. 'So when can we schedule the first appointment for the boys?'

Dr Kilshannon took a large, leather-bound diary from his briefcase and leafed through it.

'The next available space, if I make some shuffles to accommodate you, will be in,' he took out a red pen and made some adjustments to his notes, 'three months' time. November fifteenth.'

Ben and I looked at one another. I read in his eyes exactly what I knew he saw in mine.

'Thank you for your help, doctor,' he said, standing up and extending his hand. 'I think we'll just have to make our own arrangements. The need here is immediate.'

While Ben showed the bemused young psychologist out, I pulled over the file and looked again at the picture the boys had drawn during that first play session of the spectre they had seen. I looked at it for a long time. There was no help for us then. Three months was too long. The boys could not wait three months, and neither could I.

'All right, Toddy,' I said to the picture. 'You've come to us. It's our turn to go to you.'

Ben came back in and sat down opposite me.

'Well, that was a waste of time,' he said. 'I don't know why I build my hopes up every time, but I always do.'

'It's okay,' I said, putting the picture back into the file. 'I know what needs to be done.'

'Do we have a cunning plan, then?'

'We do,' I said, and told him.

'We got your report on the visit to the Byrne house,' Bríd said to me over the phone. I had been about to leave the office to go and see Mina at the hospital when the call came. 'It makes for unpleasant reading.'

'Did you expect otherwise?'

'I suppose not. I have passed a copy on to social services and to the police. I am told that a prosecution will almost certainly follow.'

'Good.'

'You may be asked to testify.'

'I have no problem with that.'

'Olwyn has asked for some time off on grounds of stress.'

'That's probably for the best.'

'Might it have been better to have brought one of the more experienced members of staff with you?'

'No. She was the best person for the job.'

'I'm afraid she may not return to us.'

'Don't underestimate her, Bríd. She's already a good childcare worker. I think she's going to be a great one. You've read the report. You know what happened. She held up pretty well under the circumstances.'

'Mmm.'

'How are Larry and Francey doing?'

'They are a little introverted, but none the worse for wear. Karena has been putting in some extra shifts, spending a lot of time with them.'

'You've got a good team, Bríd. I hope you realize it.'

'I do.'

'I dare say Olwyn will be back with you in a day or two. Give her some time. You won't regret it.'

'When will we be seeing you again?'

'I'll be out tomorrow.'

Mina smiled when I came into her room. The doctor had told me that she'd been tested for HIV, gonorrhoea, syphilis and a battery of other sexually transmitted infections. The Henrys' money had ensured a rapid response to the tests, and the results, thankfully, had all come back clear. She wasn't pregnant either. The medical staff had treated her for pubic lice as a matter of course. Mina had suffered severe vaginal bruising and some internal lacerations, but they would heal.

I had brought her flowers, some teen magazines (which I normally don't approve of, but thought I could waive my distaste just this once) and a box of chocolates.

'How are you doing, Mina?'

'Okay. Mum and Dad have just gone home to change their clothes.'

'Have they given you a hard time?'

'No. They've been really great.'

'That's good.'

'They've said that me and Jacob can see each other whenever we want.' She sat up painfully and opened the sweets. 'Want one?'

'Thanks.' I popped a hazelnut whirl in my mouth. 'Yeah, they told me about Jacob. That's really brilliant.'

'I can't wait to tell him. They're going to bring me in my phone so I can ring him.'

'I know he'll be dead chuffed to hear from you.'

'He's the best,' she said, smiling at the thought of him.

'So.' I had to bring up what had happened. 'Does that mean no more wandering? Because I almost didn't find you this time.'

'I know. I'm sorry, Shane. I didn't mean for it to go so wrong.'

'What happened, Mina? I think you owe me an explanation.'

'I don't want to talk about it. I'm tired.'

'Honey, it was bad, but it could have been an awful lot worse. I'd like to know why you were there, in that awful room with those men, in the state you were in.'

She looked away from me, towards the wall, for a while. I knew she was trying to work out where to begin. There was so much that had to be said.

'I love Jacob,' she said finally.

'I know you do.'

'But I didn't think I'd ever be allowed to be with him.

266

When I ran away first, I was trying to find where he lived. Dad had said once that Jacob's family lived in a poor part of town, so I walked until I found a place that seemed to be poor. And I asked a man I met if he knew where Jacob Benedict lived. He said he didn't, but asked if he could take me for a drink.'

'Terence Fields.'

'Yes. It was Terry.'

Sometimes fate steps in and goes out of its way to make matters considerably more messed up than they already are. I have often, when faced with the most ludicrous and unlucky coincidences that litter some of my cases, been flabbergasted at the perversity of fortune. Had Mina really just run into this predator by accident? It seemed more likely that Fields had spotted her, wandering alone by the docks, and followed until an opportunity to make contact presented itself. At any rate, this vulnerable young woman and this despicable man had, somehow, found one another in the side-streets of the city that night, and a chain of events had been set in motion.

'Tell me about him.'

'He was nice to me. He was old, and kind of ugly, and he didn't smell good, but he treated me like I was just the same as anyone else. He told me I was beautiful. *Desirable*, he said. We did things grown-ups do. We went for drinks in the pub, and to the pictures, and he let me sleep in his bed if I did . . . private . . . things with him.'

'He shouldn't have made you do those things, Mina.'

'I didn't mind, mostly. He made funny noises and shouted out my name, but he told me that this was what people who liked each other did. He said it was grown-up love. I needed to learn about it. Me and Jacob, we just kissed and hugged, but Terry did a lot more than that. It felt good.'

'Mina, that's sex. It's not love.' This is a conversation I always hate having with kids. Trying to find the correct words, being honest without sounding patronizing is never easy. Combine that with the complex business of undoing the mischief done by a sex offender, and you have a potential minefield. 'People who love one another do it, yeah, but – shit, Mina, it's complicated.' I gave up for now. She was still doped up and confused anyway.

'I know about sex. I've read about it.'

'You can catch things, and get pregnant.'

'I know all that. Terry said you have to leave it in for seven minutes to get pregnant, though, and he was never even nearly that long.'

'That's just not true. He should have been using condoms. Do you know what they are?'

'He didn't like using condoms. He said something about taking a bath with your clothes on. I didn't understand that.'

'It's just something men say. It doesn't mean anything.'

'I liked Terry. He was sort of my boyfriend. Mum and Dad wouldn't let me be with Jacob, so when I got lonely, I'd go and see Terry. When I was with him, it was just as if I didn't look like this. I was a *woman*, not a retard. So, when I ran away that last time, I went straight to him, and told him I wanted to live in his place. He was so happy. He said we'd have a party, and invite some friends over. Except all his friends were men, and they weren't nice. They all wanted to touch me, and when I asked them to stop, they wouldn't. I asked him to make them leave me alone, and he told me not to be rude; these were our guests and I should make sure they had a good time.'

'What did you do?'

'I did what they wanted. And kept doing it. It hurt, after a while, and I started to cry. They gave me drink and pills to take, and that helped, 'cause it got so as I didn't really know what was happening. Then you were there, with that man. Was he a guard?'

'No. He was a friend, someone who wanted to help.'

'They were really frightened of him. It was like he had something behind his eyes that they saw, but I couldn't.'

'I think he wanted them to see it.'

'You saved me. You and him.'

'I found you. Your mum and dad and Jacob – and you – will have to do the saving now.'

'I thought they would kill me. I think they would have eventually.'

'I don't know. It doesn't help to think of what might have happened. You should think of what *will* happen now. How to put things right. There will be times over the next while, maybe even for the rest of your life, when you'll suddenly think of what happened in that room with those men, and you'll get scared. But we'll organize someone to help you to cope with that, when it happens.'

'I'm not scared any more. And I'm not lonely. Jacob and me, we're going to be together.'

'Yes. But there's a lot of work still to do. Your mum and dad have had an awful fright too. Your relationship with them is going to change, but with change come new challenges. It isn't going to be all plain sailing.'

'No, but it'll be *honest*. Up until now it's been about lies. They've wanted me to be what I wasn't, and I've wanted them to be what they weren't. Now we can see one another as we really are. Have another sweet.'

I took one, and we forgot about such difficult issues and munched through the box of chocolates and talked about funny things that had happened at the workshop, and who was number one in the Pop Charts, and that little cottage with its vegetable garden where she and Jacob might one day live if life got simpler and easier.

Olwyn was not surprised when I sat down beside her in the Internet café. She looked as if she hadn't been sleeping much.

'Don't you have Internet access at home?' I asked her.

'Yeah.'

'So why do you do so much of your work here?'

'Gets me out of the house.'

'Isn't it expensive?'

'I'm a member. Special rates.'

'Does your mum know you're on stress leave?'

'Jesus, no. She'd freak out completely.'

There was nothing to say to that. After my conversations with Mina about her relationship with her parents, I hadn't the heart to get into a similar exchange with Olwyn.

'How've you been?'

'Oh, brilliant. I've had time to really streamline the message boards on the sites. We were getting a load of spam, y'know?'

'You know that wasn't what I meant.'

'I've decided not to go back, Shane. I'm going to go into web design. I'm really good at it. I just need to think of a way to tell my mother . . . any advice on that?'

'You did really well, at the house, Olwyn. It was tough. You held it together.'

'Yeah, I know I did okay, but, see, since then, I keep having nightmares. I can't sleep, and I can't eat, and I can't stop thinking about that bedroom and that little cupboard with the shit all over the floor and the walls.'

The tone of her voice was getting more and more high-pitched, and I knew she was about to start hyperventilating. I shushed her and put an arm around her shoulders.

'Hey, slow down. Breathe, just breathe for a second.'

She gradually got herself under control.

'Sorry. Didn't mean to lose the run of myself. I'm kind of all over the place. I just . . . just can't get my head around what Larry and Francey told us. I mean, I've been to college and I've read case studies. I know about all the awful things people do to each other. But the sheer, abject *nastiness* of what those sick fucks did to their children . . . and they didn't do it for money or to get approval from anyone else. They weren't showing off to other sick fucks. They did it for no other reason than that they wanted to. And *that's* what's killing me. The twins' lives have been destroyed because their parents just . . . felt like doing it.'

'We know that there was abuse, at least in Malachi Byrne's past. I suspect that if we were to examine Vera's childhood, we'd probably find something awful there too. But then, maybe not. There are people who are motivated by things we'll never understand.'

'I don't think I want to live in a world where that's the case. Pain like that has to have a reason.'

'It's a cliché, but sometimes bad things happen to good people – *shit happens*, as the bumper sticker says.'

'No. I can't believe that. It has to be more than just a big, twisted, cosmic joke.'

I didn't have anything useful to say. Olwyn was going through the existential crisis everyone involved in child protection experiences at some point in their lives: is there some hidden, deeper meaning behind it all, or are you just a pawn in a huge, cosmological game of chess in which there is never a winner?

'Olwyn, you're going to have to work this one out for yourself. You've had it, probably as tough as it gets, quite early in your career, and you're asking questions any intelligent person would ask. The problem is: each of us has to come up with our own answers, ones that will fit into our personal belief systems and view of the world.'

'How do *you* do it? What do you believe?'

'You don't want to know what I think.'

'Yes, I do. I'd really like to know.'

I wanted to help her, but the truth was I was fairly mixed up on this issue, and had been for a while. It was going to be hard to articulate. I took a deep breath.

'I think there is good and bad in everyone. Most of us keep the bad parts under control, and get on with our lives and generally are nice to those around us. But some people, because they were abused or neglected or hurt in some way, or sometimes because the wiring in their heads is a bit messed up, they can't keep those bad elements in check, and they hurt; and they try to deal with all that hurting by sharing it out, giving a little bit of it to this person and that person. But that doesn't work, and the hurt just keeps getting bigger, and now there's more people hurting.'

'If that's true, then we can't ever beat it. It's insurmountable.'

I shrugged. Maybe she was right.

'Could be. But, you see, I'm not trying to beat it. I know I can't change the world. I used to think I could, but I know now that I can't. That's for bigger, smarter, better people than me. What I can do is try to alleviate the hurt that I encounter. You can't make it go away, but you can help people deal with it and maybe find a way to live with it. And in time, I think it *does* go away. Eventually, little by little.'

'I don't know if I'm strong enough for this, Shane.'

'You'll get strong.'

'Will I?'

'You will. But don't get too strong, okay? You've got to keep some of the softness too, or you can't do the job. The children need the softness. When you held Larry in the shed, and cried with him and for him – that's what he'll remember, because no one ever did that for him before. No one cared enough.'

'I think I was crying for me, too.'

I patted her on the hand.

'I know. Show me what you've been doing with the websites. Maybe you can make a *Buffy* convert of me yet.'

14

I parked at the gate and opened the rear doors of the Austin for Micky and Bobby. I had been out earlier, and knew exactly where Toddy Walsh's grave was situated. The municipal graveyard was a large, sprawling affair that spread over many acres. There was a map just inside the gate which was colour-coded by year of burial, and through that I had managed to locate the general area where Toddy had been interred. It had then been a process of walking up and down the paths, examining the details on the headstones until I found the right one.

Biddy had not scrimped on the grave. A statue of an angel wielding a great broadsword, carved in black marble, stood eight feet above me. The inscription on the base of the monument said: *Thomas Walsh, loving husband. Father to Robert and Michael. With much love.* The date of his birth and death were underneath. He had been thirty years old when he died.

The boys, each holding one of my hands, walked silently through the thousands of burial markers until we stood beneath the militant angel.

'Do you know what this is, lads?' I asked them.

They shook their heads.

'This is where your daddy is buried.'

They said nothing, looking up at the winged soldier.

'Daddy idn't dead,' Bobby said, although he was beginning to look a little uncertain.

'Yeah, he told us he wadn't ready to be dead,' Micky said.

I squatted down next to them.

'No, boys. He *is* dead. This is his grave, right here. When someone dies, the people take their body – which is what's left of you after you die – and they put it into a box and then the box goes down into a big hole in the ground. They stick statues and stones and stuff on top of it, so that people will know where to come and say prayers and remember what you were like. This is where your daddy was buried after he died.'

'No,' Bobby said, a look of panic spreading across his face. 'Tha's not right!'

I took him gently by the shoulders. 'It is, Bob. You didn't go to the funeral, did you?'

'How can he be dead?' Micky asked, wringing his hands. 'He can't be, Shane.'

'Your mammy didn't want to believe it. She never told you, you just thought he'd gone away. And when he didn't arrive home, you started to play a game where he *did* come back.'

'No! It was *real*,' Micky shouted, really scared now. His small fists were bunched up and he hit me as hard as he could on the arm. 'We sees him, so we do. He calls to *me*.'

'I bet he does, Micky. In your heart he calls all the time. But he's gone, and won't be returning. I'm sorry, I really am, but that's the truth.'

'But we *sees* him,' Bobby said, breaking free of my hold and running a few steps away from me. 'He's not dead. He's our daddy and he's not gone 'way.'

They were both crying hysterically, wandering in purposeless circles here and there on the path, their grief seemingly unquenchable now that it had finally been granted release.

I sat on the edge of the vast grave and allowed them to vent. Then, when the crying had eased slightly, I went to them and scooped them both up in my arms and held them, rocking them on my knees as the sobs reduced to hiccoughs and sniffles.

'Why di'n't she tell us?' Bobby said bitterly. 'Why haven't we seen this place 'fore?'

'Your mammy thought she was doing the right thing,' I said to them as we sat in the quiet. 'You were very little and she didn't think you'd be able to understand. The problem was: you never got the chance to say goodbye. How could he be gone when he never told you goodbye?'

'He never said 'bye to us,' Micky said. 'He was just goned.'

'We never said 'bye t' him either,' Bobby said.

'You can say goodbye now,' I said gently. 'This is where he's buried. Right where we're sitting. So if you want to say anything to him, you can.'

'Will he hear us?' Bobby said, his voice muffled by my shoulder.

'Yeah, I think he will. It's not like before, where you thought he was answering back. Real life isn't like that. But he can hear you. You can tell him what you think and what you feel.'

The two brothers pushed themselves up, their eyes red and cheeks flushed from crying, and, hand in hand, turned to the grave. They looked so small and dejected, but I was filled with pride for them. This was a hugely difficult thing they were doing. I couldn't help – they had to do it alone.

'Daddy,' Bobby said haltingly. 'Daddy, we didn't know you was dead.'

'We weren't 'lowed come when they put ya in the box and down in the ground,' Micky said. 'That's why we never said bye-bye.'

'But our friend Shane brunged us here, so's we could see you,' Bobby said. 'An' we'd like to come see ya 'gain. Maybe Mammy could bring us sometime. I think she misses you a lot. We misses you.'

'I love you, Daddy,' Micky said.

'I love you, Dad,' Bobby said.

And I fancied that I heard a sigh, then, as something was released – a ghost finally laid to rest.

Benjamin Tyrrell and I stood in a small complex of duplexes as Sylvie unpacked her few belongings from the boot of Ben's old jeep. A woman in her late fifties with grey hair tied back into a ponytail, wearing sombre colours, was helping her. She was Bernadette, a nun with the Sisters of Perpetual Solace. One of her colleagues held Gloria while they worked.

'I don't like this, Ben. Not one little bit,' I said out of the corner of my mouth.

'That's your prejudices talking,' Ben said. 'I've known Bernie for years, and she is a woman of the utmost integrity. I don't agree with her religious beliefs, and she doesn't agree with my politics, but I am telling you that Sylvie will be safe and extremely well supported here. I would not have suggested it if I didn't think she and the little one would be okay.'

'I'll be keeping a *very* close eye on things.'

'That's up to you. But trust me, will you? This is the best possible solution. She gets to keep Gloria, have her own place, and be given all the help she needs. There's proper security, so if her father does come back and finds her, he won't be able to gain access. Her movements will be closely monitored, so the temptation of going back onto the streets is considerably lessened. This is as good as it gets, Shane.'

Sylvie and Gloria had a two-bedroom upstairs flat. A family support worker would visit daily, and one of the sisters would be on call round the clock. Childcare was available, and Sylvie would be returning to school in September. I helped her put her things away while Ben went for coffee with Bernadette. When we had finished and the place was a little more like home, she made us a pot of tea.

'Well, this is nice, isn't it?' I asked.

She nodded, looking bothered.

'What's up?'

'It's . . . I dunno, it's nearly *too* good. Stuff like this, it doesn't happen to me. I mean, I've got my own place, someone's going to come in to help me every day, they're sending me back to school and paying for the childcare. Shit, Shane, it's like every dream I've had over the past few years has all come true. The last time that happened, it all got fucked up real fast, y'know what I'm sayin'?'

'Yeah, I know. But this is different. Ben knows these people, and he swears they're genuine. I'm going to be stopping by a lot, and if there's any problems, you let me know. I think you've fallen on your feet here, babe.'

She smiled and took my hand in hers. Gloria was jabbering away contentedly on the floor, playing with a set of coloured blocks Ben had brought for her.

'You made this happen.'

'Ben made it happen.'

'No, you found me again. You came back and you got me. My minder.'

I smiled, feeling a sudden tug deep inside. 'You haven't called me that in a long time.'

'I know. I remembered you, when you came that first night by the docks. I just didn't say, 'cause I thought you were there for . . . for something bad. But I remembered. You used to read me *Cinderella*. I'd ask you about fairy godmothers.'

'I told you I hoped they were real.'

'All I wanted, back then, was to have my daddy come and get me. I used to imagine what he was like, and all the things we'd do together when he came for me. I was so stupid.'

'No, you weren't stupid. Every child in care has those dreams.'

'I stopped dreaming, you know, for a while. It hurt too much, and I kind of stopped caring about me. I wasn't worth it. But then Gloria came, and I started to dream again, for her. I began to wish for that fairy godmother you used to read to me about, that she'd appear in a puff of smoke and make all the bad things go away so that we could have a life. And then you came back. After all those years, *you came back*. And I had more than dreams. I had hope.'

'There's always hope. Even that fairy godmothers might be real.'

'I think, maybe, they are, but they come in two types: fairy godmothers and fairy godfathers.'

'D'you reckon?'

'Yeah. I know which kind I've got.'

I never got to testify on behalf of Larry and Francey. I was ready: I had rehearsed carefully what I was going to say. The lawyer for the Health Executive had gone over all the possible questions I would be asked, examining the revelations made by the children from every conceivable angle. On the day of the trial, I dressed in a linen suit, combed my hair and drove to the courthouse, feeling positive. There was no way Malachi and Vera Byrne could walk away from this.

I was met at the door of the main building by Marcus, the Health Executive's lawyer. He was a blond-haired, tanned young man, muscular and a little over six feet tall. He affected a slacker, surfer patois that seemed at odds with his chosen profession.

'You might as well have stayed at home, bro,' he said, leading me to a bench just inside the lobby. 'It's over already.'

'What do you mean?'

'Mr Byrne has pleaded guilty to the whole shooting match. All that's left is the sentencing, which won't happen today. You can go home.'

'Hang on, Marcus, slow down a second. Malachi Byrne has admitted to it all?'

'Everything that was on the table, man. Dude signed a statement last night. He's already been taken into custody.'

I was bowled over. It didn't make sense. Why would he have done such a thing? Logic suggested that he may have wanted to prevent the children any further pain by stopping the case from going to trial, but I knew him better than that. Mercy was not a part of his make-up. Then, in a flash of understanding, I knew.

'You say Malachi signed a statement. What about Vera?'

'She's in the clear. He's admitted to coercing her, taken the fall for everything. She walks.'

For a second, I thought I was going to faint. I felt a great chasm open up beneath me. She had double-crossed us all. Malachi Byrne was cruel and vicious and spiteful, but he verged on having an intellectual disability. Vera was the head of the serpent. It was she who was the really guilty one, who had done the coercing. And she had got away with all of it.

'You okay, dude? You look like you're about to hurl.'

I stood up, walked as fast as I could to the door and threw my breakfast up all over a potted plant.

Bríd sat at her desk, looking tired. Even her Afro seemed half-hearted.

'Yes, I got the news this morning, probably while you were on your way to court. I don't know what to say, Shane. I agree that this is a far from ideal outcome. But at least one of them will see the inside of a prison.'

'That's hardly the point. Vera Byrne was the real abuser. She masterminded the whole fucking thing, was behind every torture they experienced. Malachi was a blunt instrument she used – nothing more. How are the twins going to feel when they hear? It's another insult, one more example of how worthless they are.' I suddenly realized I was shouting, and stopped, feeling embarrassed.

'What do you want me to say? I wish I could make it different.'

'She's dangerous, Bríd. She wants them, and she'll stop at nothing until she has them. She must *never* get them back.'

'I know.'

I nodded. 'Good.'

Larry, Francey and Olwyn were sitting on the grass in front of the house, looking at a book. I went out to them, slinging my jacket over my shoulder.

'Hey,' Olwyn said.

I sat down.

'I need to talk to you, kids,' I said. 'It's important.'

They put down the book and turned to face me.

'I was down at the courthouse just now. Do you know what a court is?'

''Swhere they puts bad peoples in jail,' Francey said, then laughed. 'They puttin' you in jail?'

'No. I was supposed to be talking to the judge about your mum and dad.'

'Oh,' Larry said. 'Yeah, they telled us they was goin' t' be puttin' Mam an' Dad away, a'righ'.'

'Well, they have put your father in prison. But see, he told the judge everything that happened was his fault, and because of that, your mum maybe won't be going to jail.'

The children looked at one another.

'She made Daddy say dat,' Francey said solemnly. 'He always does what'n'ever she says.'

'I knewed she wasn' goin' in no jail,' Larry said, sighing. Neither of them seemed surprised by this turn of events. It was almost as if they had always expected this was how it would go. 'Even if they putted her in, she wouldn' stay. She'd 'scape.'

'I don't know about that, Larry, but anyway, she's not going to jail. I just wanted you to know.'

'When can we see her?' Francey asked.

I was taken aback by the question.

'Do you want to see her?'

'I kinda miss 'er.'

'Me too,' Larry said.

I looked at Olwyn, who had an expression of horror on her face.

'Um, I'll talk to Bríd about setting up some access visits, I suppose,' I said.

The bond of blood: it never ceases to amaze me. No matter how abhorrent the abuse, it abides. Vera Byrne, for all her sadism and menace, was still their mother.

She answered the door to me before I even knocked.

'I knew you'd come,' she said. 'I'd guess we'll be seein' a lot more of one another now.'

'What are you up to, Vera?'

'I'm the innocent victim of years of harsh treatment. You should feel sorry for me.'

'Cut the crap. You've managed to swing this, but don't think you've achieved a damn thing. I am going to make it my personal mission to see you behind bars, one way or another. The police already have my report. I'll talk to your neighbours in Oldtown, go to the hall of records and find out about your relatives, and speak to them. Every single thing the twins say when I'm with them, I'll write down. I *will* have you.'

'Oh, careful, now. Statements like that can come back to haunt you.'

'I don't know what you mean, Vera. It's just you and me here. Do you have a tape recorder?'

She smirked. 'Not this time. But there'll be others. Just be careful, is all I'm saying. I'm giving you fair warning.'

'Your children want me to arrange access visits. It's their right, and, seeing as you've been cleared of all guilt, there's nothing I can do to prevent it. But listen carefully. If they become even the slightest bit upset before, during or after a visit, I will pull the plug.'

Before I could move, her clawed hand shot out and grabbed the front of my shirt. I felt her nails scratching and cutting the skin on my chest, and then she was nose to nose with me. Fire danced in her eyes and her hot, rancid breath blasted me full in the face.

'You don't know what you're messin' with, boy. You will not keep me from seein' my twins, and you will not stop me from gettin' 'em back, either. It won't be long now, 'cause the threat is gone, all safely locked up. And

I can play *real nice*. I bet you think I'm so ugly and frightful, no one would ever trust me, but guess what? This afternoon, I'm off into town to buy a lovely dress. Then I'm going to get a facial, and I might just organize a visit to the dentist. I have a medical card and a modest little pension now my man's behind bars. I can afford to treat meself.'

I pulled away from her, but she was stronger than she looked and I had to wrestle her hand off me, cutting myself even worse in the process. She put the bloodied fingers into her mouth, sucking them loudly.

'When I show up to see Larry and Francey, I'll look like a new woman. No longer under the influence of that brute I married. I can start to rebuild my relationship with them, and we can put all this unpleasantness behind us.'

I backed away from her.

'I'm not the only one who knows what you are, Vera,' I said. 'You can't keep the act up for ever. You'll slip, and when you do, I'll be there.'

'Ah, don't be such a spoilsport. Don't we all deserve a second chance?' she said, and laughing heartily, closed the door.

'How do I look?' Mina asked me for the tenth time.

'You look great.'

'You're a man. You'd say that anyway.'

'Why do you keep asking me, then?'

'I want to look really lovely. They wouldn't let him come into the hospital. He hasn't seen me in three weeks.'

She pulled down the sun visor on the passenger side,

which had a mirror set into it, and teased a piece of hair.

'Mina, please believe me, you look stunning. He is a very lucky young man.'

'Really?'

'Really.'

I turned onto Garibaldi Street and parked outside the Henrys' house.

'Now,' I said, shutting off the engine. 'How are you feeling?'

'I feel brilliant.'

'No dizziness or sickness?'

'None. I haven't had any in a week, Shane. Stop fussing.'

'Okay. Well, let's go.'

She reached over and hugged me tight for a moment, giving me a kiss on the cheek, then opened the door and got out.

Standing at the front door of the house was Molly. Beside her, wearing a fluorescent green suit with an electric-red shirt and a pink bowtie, and clutching the biggest bunch of flowers he could physically carry, was Jacob. Mina ran to him, laughing and crying all at the same time, and planted a huge kiss on his forehead. He was grinning from ear to ear and flushed with pride and embarrassment. Arm in arm, they walked away together, up the street.

Molly had a handkerchief out and was dabbing at the tears running down her cheeks. Dirk was noticeable for his absence.

'You're doing the right thing,' I said, coming to stand with her.

'Will they be all right?' she asked. 'They have so much stacked against them.'

'They're not moving to Alaska. Mina's not moving out at all. What they're doing is being a couple, out in the open and without shame. I've had a long talk with Jacob, given him a sense of what happened to her and told him to treat her gently for a while. She might tell him about it herself, or she may not. It's up to her. Where's your husband?'

'Dirk has found this very hard.'

'She needs you both. Don't let this tear you apart as a family.'

'We won't. He's a good man. He's just proud. He loves her so very much.'

'I know. But he should be showing her, now more than ever. And he has to let her have some freedom.'

'I think she is free. Perhaps for the first time.'

We stood in the sunshine and watched the two of them disappear around the corner.

'Do you think they'll make it?' Molly asked me.

'They already have,' I said.

Benjamin Tyrrell was sitting in my chair when I got back to the office that evening, his feet up on my desk.

'Your probationary period is up,' he said.

'I know. School starts back next week. I was wondering when you'd bring it up.'

'Well,' he said, putting his hands behind his head, 'I think you did pretty well, despite a few hiccoughs. The Walshes are in good shape. The Henrys are on the road to recovery. The Byrne case is likely to remain open for some time longer, but that was out of anyone's control, and you advanced our understanding of it considerably. Your own little project, Sylvie, was concluded satisfactorily, even if I do say so myself. All in all, a fine couple of months' work.'

'Are you firing me, or saying that there's a position here for me if I want one?'

'I do believe I am offering you a job.'

'I've heard that there are easier ways to make a living.'

'Naw. This is where it's at. Glamour, excitement, wage packets stuffed to bursting at the end of the week . . .'

'I suppose you have my cases lined up already.'

'Wanna hear about them?'

'No. Buy me a pint instead. We can talk about them tomorrow.'

He stood up. I held the door as he walked out.

'Suppose I should get you a set of keys cut.'

'Suppose you should.'

And I pulled the door of Last Ditch House closed for the night.

Afterword

My previous book, *Wednesday's Child*, dealt with three, standard child-protection cases. They were all unique and special, and the children involved were all exceptional people, but social-care workers who have read the book have all recognized elements of those stories in cases they have been involved with (in fact, one social worker in a region of Ireland I have never visited, let alone practised in, was absolutely convinced I was writing about one of her cases, despite the fact that I have never met her or the family to which she was referring).

Crying in the Dark does not deal with the usual. I purposely set out to focus on four cases with details that were slightly out of the ordinary. They are stories I tend to use to illustrate points when teaching, as they each hold a fundamental message about children and how amazingly resilient they are, and about just how strange this work can get. Because it *can* get strange at times.

The story of Micky and Bobby Walsh happened exactly as I describe it here. They really did believe they were meeting their dead father down the back of the garden, and that line drawing I have reproduced is pretty much what they drew for me. All the odd things that occurred in that house did happen. Was I encountering supernatural forces? I have spent years asking myself that question. When someone tells you that there is a ghost in a house, whether you believe them or not, you begin to interpret things in ways you normally would not. I am a social scientist, with several degrees to my name, but I am human, and as open to suggestion as the next man. I am quite happy to believe (and in the dead of the night, this is what I tell myself) that what I experienced were a few freak weather conditions, a wobbly stool and a couple of deeply distressed little boys. As for branches that weren't there scratching at windows, well, all houses have their own idiosyncratic noises, don't they? I've left it open: you decide. Suffice it to say that, after we visited the grave and those two amazing children said their goodbyes, the visitations stopped. Bobby and Micky are two happy, well-adjusted adolescents now, and their house looks a lot less like a shrine than it once did.

Mina and Jacob did not remain a couple (wouldn't it have been lovely if they had), but she is now working in a job she loves outside the workshop system, and has a long-term partner.

Do people like Karl Devereux really exist? Yes, they do, particularly in the field of youth and community work. I have, in fact, been in community centres completely run by ex-prisoners. This should not come as a real surprise. These men and women have paid their debt to society (personally, I don't believe that prison should be about debt collection, but that's another story), and have life experiences that can be invaluable to young people who may be immersed in gang culture or living on the periphery of organized crime. These people have true insights into the workings of aspects of society the rest of us *cannot* have. I come from a working-class background, but

I've never been beaten or abused or starved. Individuals like Devereux – men who choose each word they speak with care, because in prison, a slip of the tongue can get you beaten up or killed – have, and they bring that experience with them into their interactions with young people, and meet them on a level the rest of us cannot.

Larry and Francey were not feral children in the strictest sense of the word, but they certainly had feral aspects (those of you interested in reading more about feral children should have a look at Douglas Candland's book *Feral Children and Clever Animals*, published by Oxford University Press). Their father was sentenced to four years in prison, and he served around a year and a half of that. Their mother never served one single day of a custodial sentence, despite the fact that she was the motivating force behind the abuse, and that all the reports and evidence furnished to the court stated this clearly. Unfortunately, female perpetrators of abuse usually slip through the system, primarily because our society still does not recognize them as a real threat. Men abuse, the accepted wisdom states. Women are victims.

I ran into Sylvie Lambe fourteen months ago, purely by accident. I scarcely recognized her, but she knew me straight away and bounded over, full of confidence and good humour. She is a tall, strikingly beautiful young woman in her twenties now, who has left her past far behind her. My initial reticence about putting her in the care of a religious order was, thankfully, totally misplaced. She now works as part of an outreach programme with the Sisters, and has developed a deep spirituality: when I met her, she was just back from a pilgrimage to Lough

Derg. She is still a single mother, but Gloria is a constant source of joy in her life, and the right man, she told me, would have to win over two women. We reminisced about old, darker times, and I was humbled by the fact that she harbours no bitterness. After ten minutes or so she gave me a hug, promised to keep in touch, and was gone into the bustle of the city streets. I knew I wouldn't hear from her until she accidentally wandered into my life again. I was outgrown a long time ago. And that is okay. The work I do is about facilitating growth, and that means charting the trajectory of a life for a time, and then watching it flame away into the ether, creating a new and beautiful course all of its own – strong, independent and free.

Acknowledgements

Thanks are to due to many people who were instrumental in the writing of this book:

Jonathan Williams, my agent, was once again the first person to read the text, and his editorial comments, support and friendship have been a huge benefit to me over the past couple of years. Jonathan, you have made me a better writer.

All the staff in Gill & Macmillan have been enthusiastic, warm and nurturing: Fergal, Sinéad, Dearbhla, D and everyone else, many thanks.

Darren Giddens, who advised on early drafts, has been my friend since we first happened across one another in a classroom in Waterford Regional Technical College in 1991. Thanks for everything, Darren.

John Connolly, a great writer and a true friend, was good enough to read a first draft and offer much needed support during a moment of doubt. Thanks for your time and encouragement, John.

Andy Irvine, who has been an inspiration to me for many years (for his wonderful social conscience as much as his remarkable musicianship), kindly gave permission for the use of *As I Roved Out*. Cheers, Andy.

This book was written in a variety of locations, mostly during the generous breaks we teachers get during the year. Particular thanks are due to Phil, Ted, Gráinne,

Fergus and Edel, in whose home in Meath, closeted away in the living room, I wrote quite a bit of the text and consumed copious cups of tea. My little sister, Tara, and her partner, Gerry, also welcomed me into their Dublin apartment one Hallowe'en, during which time Mina Henry made her first appearance in print.

My students (and there are too many of you to mention), as well as being a constant source of inspiration and friendship, have been so incredibly supportive of me since this whole business began, that I simply do not have the words to express my gratitude. I have received letters and cards from past students, words of encouragement and congratulations at every turn. I don't deserve you all. Thanks.

Deirdre, Richard and Marnie have the job of living with me on a daily basis, a job that becomes quite challenging when I'm reaching the final stages of a manuscript. I love you all, and thank you for putting up with the impatience and moods.

All the children, all the stories described in this book, are real. The experience of working with each of you has enriched my life. Thanks are owed to every one of you.

I wish to dedicate this book to two men who probably had more to do with forming me as a childcare worker, and indeed a teacher, than anyone else. There are liberal sprinklings of each of them in Ben Tyrrell, and they are mentors I return to constantly for advice and wisdom, never going away empty-handed. John and Damien, this book is for you.